Google Cloud Platform for Developers

A Step-by-Step Approach to GCP

THOMPSON CARTER

Table of Content

TABLE OF CONTENTS

8

INTRODUCTION

MASTERING GOOGLE CLOUD PLATFORM FOR DEVELOPERS

Why This Book?

The world of software development is evolving rapidly, and **cloud computing** has become a **fundamental skill** for developers, DevOps engineers, data scientists, and IT professionals. Whether you're building web applications, handling massive datasets, or scaling machine learning models, **Google Cloud Platform (GCP) provides the tools and infrastructure to do it efficiently and securely**.

However, **navigating cloud technologies can be overwhelming**—especially with the vast range of services, configurations, and best practices available. That's where this book comes in.

Who   is   this   book   for?
Beginners – Learn the fundamentals of Google Cloud with

hands-on   tutorials.
Experienced Developers – Master advanced topics like Kubernetes, AI, and DevOps pipelines.
Cloud Architects & DevOps Engineers – Design scalable and cost-efficient cloud solutions.
Data Scientists & AI Engineers – Harness GCP's AI/ML tools to build smart applications.

This book is designed to be **jargon-free** and filled with **real-world examples** so you can **apply what you learn immediately**. By the end, you'll be **confidently deploying, managing, and scaling applications on GCP** like a pro.

What You Will Learn in This Book

This book is structured into **four parts**, gradually guiding you from cloud fundamentals to advanced real-world implementations.

Part 1: Getting Started with Google Cloud

In this section, we introduce **Google Cloud Platform (GCP)**, compare it with other cloud providers like AWS and Azure, and set up your first cloud project. You'll learn about:

GCP Console & CLI – Navigating and managing cloud services   efficiently.

IAM & Security – Managing users, permissions, and access   controls.

Compute, Storage, and Networking Basics – Key services like Compute Engine, Cloud Storage, and Virtual Private Cloud (VPC).

By the end of this section, you'll have a **fully configured GCP environment ready for development**.

Part 2: Deploying Applications & Managing Workloads

Once you're comfortable with the fundamentals, it's time to **build and deploy applications on GCP**. This section covers:

Compute Engine & Kubernetes Engine (GKE) – Running applications on VMs and containers.

Serverless Computing – Deploying apps with **Cloud Functions, Cloud Run, and App Engine**.

Storage & Databases – Managing structured and unstructured data with Cloud SQL, Firestore, and BigQuery.

By the end of this section, you'll know **how to build, scale, and deploy cloud-native applications using Google Cloud**.

Part 3: DevOps, Automation, and AI/ML on GCP

Modern cloud applications require **automation, monitoring, and AI-driven intelligence**. This section focuses on:

CI/CD Pipelines with Cloud Build – Automating software deployment.

Infrastructure as Code (IaC) with Terraform – Managing infrastructure efficiently.

Monitoring & Security Best Practices – Using Cloud Operations Suite (Stackdriver) for logging and incident response.

AutoML & AI Predictions – Enhancing applications with machine learning models.

By the end of this section, you'll be able to **automate infrastructure, optimize deployments, and integrate AI into your applications**.

Part 4: Scaling, Optimization, and Career Growth

To wrap things up, this section focuses on:
Cost Optimization Strategies – Reducing cloud costs while maintaining performance.
Disaster Recovery & High Availability – Ensuring business continuity.
Future Trends in Cloud Computing – Preparing for innovations like **serverless, edge computing, and AI-driven automation**.
Career Growth & Certifications – How to get Google Cloud certified and advance your cloud career.

By the end of this section, you'll not only **master Google Cloud Platform** but also **understand how to optimize costs, maintain security, and stay ahead in your career**.

Why Google Cloud?

There are many cloud providers, but **Google Cloud has become a top choice** for developers due to:

Global-Scale Infrastructure – Used by companies like YouTube, Spotify, and Twitter.
Cutting-Edge AI/ML Services – Industry-leading AI models and AutoML capabilities.

Strong Kubernetes & Serverless Support – Google pioneered Kubernetes and serverless computing.
Best-in-Class Security – Advanced security features like IAM, encryption, and DLP.
Powerful Data & Analytics Tools – BigQuery, Dataflow, and AI-driven insights.

This book is **not just about learning Google Cloud**—it's about understanding **how to leverage it to build powerful, scalable, and cost-effective applications**.

Hands-On, Real-World Approach

Theory is important, but practical knowledge is what makes you a cloud expert.

This book emphasizes **hands-on learning** through:
Step-by-step tutorials – Walkthroughs to help you deploy services in Google Cloud.
Real-world case studies – Learn from how top companies use GCP.
Code examples & configurations – Ready-to-use snippets for quick implementation.

Interactive exercises – Test what you've learned at the end of each chapter.

By the time you finish this book, you'll be **ready to tackle real-world cloud challenges** and **deploy production-grade applications with confidence**.

How to Get the Most Out of This Book

Follow Along with Hands-On Labs – Set up a free-tier GCP account and practice. **Experiment with Real Cloud Projects** – Build applications, automate infrastructure, and test cloud security. **Join Google Cloud Developer Communities** – Network with cloud engineers and stay updated. **Pursue Google Cloud Certifications** – Validate your expertise and boost your career.

The best way to learn cloud computing is by doing!

Final Thoughts: Your Journey to Cloud Mastery Starts Now

Cloud computing is not just the future—it's the present. Mastering **Google Cloud Platform** opens up endless opportunities, from **building next-gen applications** to **solving global-scale problems with AI and automation**.

This book is your **step-by-step guide** to becoming a **skilled Google Cloud developer**. Whether you're aiming to **pass certification exams, launch a startup, or scale enterprise applications**, this book will give you the **knowledge, tools, and confidence** to succeed.

 Are you ready to become a Google Cloud expert? Let's dive in and start building the future—one cloud deployment at a time.

Part 1

Getting Started with Google Cloud

CHAPTER 1

Introduction to Google Cloud Platform (GCP)

1.1 The Evolution of Cloud Computing

In the past, businesses relied on **physical servers** housed in on-premise data centers. Scaling up meant buying new servers, configuring them manually, and managing maintenance. This **time-consuming and costly approach** led to the **rise of cloud computing**, allowing businesses to access computing power, storage, and services **on demand**.

Today, **cloud platforms like Google Cloud Platform (GCP), Amazon Web Services (AWS), and Microsoft Azure** have revolutionized software development, enabling companies to deploy applications faster, scale effortlessly, and reduce operational overhead.

Why Cloud Computing Matters:

- Eliminates **hardware limitations**—resources are available whenever needed.

- Enables **pay-as-you-go pricing**—pay only for what you use.
- Offers **global reach**—deploy apps closer to users for better performance.
- Ensures **automatic backups and disaster recovery**—data stays secure.

Google Cloud Platform (GCP) has emerged as **one of the leading cloud providers**, offering a **developer-friendly, AI-powered, and security-focused** cloud environment.

1.2 What is Google Cloud Platform?

Google Cloud Platform (GCP) is a **suite of cloud computing services** that runs on **Google's infrastructure**, the same infrastructure that powers Google Search, YouTube, and Gmail.

Key Features of GCP:

Compute Power – Run virtual machines, containers, and serverless   apps.

Storage Solutions – Store files, databases, and large datasets   efficiently.

Machine Learning & AI – Use pre-trained AI models or build custom ones.

Networking – Scale your apps globally with Google's high-speed network.

Security & Compliance – Benefit from Google's enterprise-grade security.

Why Developers Choose GCP:
Developer-Friendly: GCP offers **one-click deployments**, a **powerful command-line interface (gcloud)**, and **built-in DevOps tools** for automation.
Best-in-Class AI/ML Services: Google's AI tools like **AutoML, Vertex AI, and TensorFlow** simplify **AI-driven development**.
Sustainable & Carbon Neutral: Google Cloud is **100% powered by renewable energy**, making it the most **eco-friendly** cloud provider.

GCP vs. AWS vs. Azure: What Makes Google Cloud Unique?

Feature	Google Cloud (GCP)	Amazon Web Services (AWS)	Microsoft Azure
Strengths	AI/ML, Big Data, Kubernetes	Largest service catalog, mature ecosystem	Enterprise integrations (Microsoft 365, Hybrid Cloud)
Ease of Use	Simplified UI & strong automation	Complex setup, but powerful	Best for enterprises using Windows
Networking	High-performance, low-latency **global fiber network**	Broad global infrastructure	Strong hybrid networking
Pricing Model	**Sustained use discounts**, per-second billing	Volume-based pricing	Reserved instances for cost savings

Who Should Use Google Cloud?

- **Startups & developers** looking for an easy-to-use cloud with AI/ML tools.

30

- **Data-driven companies** that need real-time analytics & big data processing.
- **Enterprises** looking for a **scalable**, secure, and **cost-effective** alternative to AWS and Azure.

1.3 Understanding Cloud Computing Models: IaaS, PaaS, SaaS

Before diving into **GCP services**, it's important to understand the **three primary cloud computing models**:

Infrastructure as a Service (IaaS)

What it is: Provides virtual machines, storage, and networking.

Example in GCP: Compute Engine (VMs on demand).

Use Case: You need full control over the OS, storage, and networking.

Real-world Example: A company moving from physical servers to virtual machines on GCP's **Compute Engine** to scale workloads on demand.

Platform as a Service (PaaS)

What it is: Provides a platform to develop, run, and manage apps without dealing with infrastructure.
Example in GCP: App Engine (serverless application hosting).
Use Case: You want to deploy applications without managing the backend.
Real-world Example: A startup launches a **web app using App Engine**, allowing it to scale automatically without worrying about server maintenance.

Software as a Service (SaaS)

What it is: Ready-to-use software hosted on the cloud.
Example in GCP: Google Workspace (Gmail, Drive, Docs).
Use Case: You need a tool that is fully managed and ready to use.
Real-world Example: A **remote-first company** using Google Meet, Drive, and Docs for collaboration without needing IT management.

Key Takeaway: GCP provides all three models, allowing developers to choose **the right level of control vs. automation** for their needs.

1.4 Real-World Example: How Startups Use GCP to Scale Fast

Case Study: A Startup Migrating to GCP for Cost Savings & Performance

Imagine a **fast-growing startup** that builds a **video streaming platform** similar to YouTube. Initially, they host everything **on-premise**, but as they grow:

- Their servers **struggle to handle traffic spikes**.
- They **pay too much** for maintenance and electricity.
- Security concerns arise as **user data increases**.

How GCP Helped:
Compute Engine & Kubernetes Engine: The startup moves its **backend to Kubernetes (GKE)** for auto-scaling.
Cloud Storage & CDN: Stores video files efficiently with **Cloud Storage** and speeds up content delivery with **Cloud CDN**.
BigQuery for Analytics: Uses **BigQuery** to analyze **user engagement and video performance**.
AI-Powered Recommendations: Integrates **Vertex AI** to **recommend videos based on user behavior**.

Results:

- **90% reduction in maintenance costs**—no more hardware purchases.
- **Auto-scalability**—handles **1 million users without downtime**.
- **AI-driven engagement**—better recommendations improve retention.

Lesson: Startups love GCP because it offers flexibility, cost savings, and built-in AI tools.

1.5 Summary: Why Learn Google Cloud?

Google Cloud is an **essential skill** for developers, DevOps engineers, and IT professionals. **Whether you're launching a startup, managing enterprise workloads, or working with AI and big data, GCP offers powerful tools to streamline development.**

Key Takeaways from Chapter 1: Google Cloud **powers global applications** like YouTube, Gmail, and Google Search. GCP offers **compute, storage, AI, networking, and security** services.

Compared to AWS & Azure, **GCP excels in AI/ML, Kubernetes, and cost optimization**. Understanding **IaaS, PaaS, and SaaS** helps you choose the **right GCP service**. **Real-world businesses** use GCP to scale, save costs, and innovate faster.

What's   Next?
In the next chapter, we'll **set up your first GCP account, explore the free tier, and launch your first cloud resource**.

Next Chapter: Setting Up Your GCP Account
Learn   how   to:
Create a **free-tier GCP account** and access **$300 in free credits**.

Use the **GCP Console and gcloud CLI** to manage cloud resources.

Deploy your **first virtual machine in Compute Engine**.

Let's get hands-on with Google Cloud!

CHAPTER 2

Setting Up Your GCP Account

2.1 Getting Started with Google Cloud

Now that you understand **what Google Cloud Platform (GCP) is and why it matters**, it's time to **get hands-on**. In this chapter, you'll learn how to: **Create a free-tier GCP account** and access **$300 in free credits**.

Navigate the GCP console and use the command-line interface (gcloud CLI). **Understand GCP pricing models and avoid unexpected costs.**

Deploy your first Virtual Machine (VM) using Compute Engine.

By the end of this chapter, you'll have a **fully functional GCP account** and will have deployed your **first cloud resource**.

2.2 Creating a Free Tier GCP Account

Google Cloud offers **a free-tier account** with **$300 in free credits** for new users. This allows you to **experiment with GCP services** without worrying about costs.

Step-by-Step: Creating a GCP Account

Go to the GCP Signup Page:

- Visit **https://cloud.google.com/free**.

Sign in with a Google Account:

- You'll need a **Google account (Gmail) to proceed**.

Set Up Billing Information:

- Enter your billing details **(credit/debit card required for verification, but you won't be charged).**
- Google offers **$300 free credits valid for 90 days**.

Agree to Terms & Create Your Account:

- Once completed, you'll be redirected to the **Google Cloud Console**.

Pro Tip: If you're a **student**, check out **Google Cloud for Students** for additional credits.

2.3 Navigating the Google Cloud Console & CLI

Using the GCP Console

The **Google Cloud Console** is a **web-based dashboard** where you can manage your cloud resources.

Key Sections in the Console:

- **Navigation Menu (☰)** → Access all GCP services.
- **Billing** → View costs and manage budgets.
- **IAM & Admin** → Manage user access and permissions.
- **Cloud Shell** → A browser-based terminal to run `gcloud` commands.

Using the gcloud CLI

The **gcloud command-line interface (CLI)** allows you to **interact with GCP using terminal commands**.

Installing gcloud CLI:

1. Download the SDK from **https://cloud.google.com/sdk/docs/install**.
2. Run the installer and follow the setup instructions.
3. Authenticate with your Google Cloud account:

```sh
gcloud auth login
```

4. Set your default project:

```sh
gcloud config set project [PROJECT_ID]
```

Why Use gcloud? Faster than navigating the console. Automate deployments & resource management. Use scripting for repetitive tasks.

2.4 Understanding Pricing Models & Cost Estimation

How Google Cloud Pricing Works

Google Cloud follows a **pay-as-you-go** model. You are charged based on **actual resource usage** (e.g., compute power, storage, network traffic).

Key   Pricing   Concepts:
Sustained Use Discounts – Save up to **30% on VMs** that run   continuously.
Preemptible VMs – Save **up to 80%** by using **temporary, low-cost   VMs**.
Free Tier Services – Many services, like **Cloud Functions and Firestore**, offer **free quotas**.

Estimating Costs Before Deploying

Use the **GCP Pricing Calculator**:

- Go to **https://cloud.google.com/pricing/calculator**.
- Select services like **Compute Engine, Cloud Storage, and BigQuery**.
- Get an **estimated monthly cost** before deployment.

Pro Tip: Set up a budget alert in the **Billing Dashboard** to avoid unexpected charges.

2.5 Hands-on Tutorial: Deploying Your First VM in Compute Engine

Now, let's **deploy your first virtual machine (VM)** in Google Cloud using Compute Engine.

What is Compute Engine?

Compute Engine is GCP's **Infrastructure-as-a-Service (IaaS) offering**, allowing you to **create and manage virtual machines (VMs)**.

Why Use Compute Engine?

- Runs any OS (Linux, Windows).
- Scalable and customizable.
- Supports GPU acceleration for AI/ML workloads.

Step 1: Create a Virtual Machine (VM) via the Console

Go to Compute Engine:

- In the **GCP Console**, navigate to **Compute Engine →
VM instances**.

41

Click "Create Instance".

Configure Your VM:

- **Name:** `my-first-vm`
- **Region & Zone:** Choose the closest data center (e.g., `us-central1-a`).
- **Machine Type:** Choose **e2-micro (free-tier eligible)**.
- **Boot Disk:** Select **Debian Linux (default)**.

Click "Create" to launch your VM!

Your VM is now running on Google Cloud!

Step 2: Connect to the VM via SSH

Click the "SSH" button next to your VM in the console. A terminal window will open inside your browser. Run a test command:

```sh

uname -a
```

This will display the Linux kernel version running on your VM.

You have successfully accessed your VM!

Step 3: Deploying a Simple Web Server on Your VM

Let's install **Nginx**, a popular web server.

Update the package manager:

```sh
sudo apt update
```

Install Nginx:

```sh
sudo apt install nginx -y
```

Start Nginx:

```sh
sudo systemctl start nginx
```

Check if Nginx is running:

```sh
```

```
systemctl status nginx
```

You should see **Nginx is active (running).**

Open your browser and visit your VM's external IP address:

```sh
```

```
echo "Hello from GCP!" | sudo tee
/var/www/html/index.html
```

Now, open:

```cpp
```

```
http://[YOUR_VM_EXTERNAL_IP]
```

🎉 **You should see "Hello from GCP!" displayed in your browser!**

2.6 Summary: Your First Steps in GCP

Congratulations! You have successfully:
Created a **Google Cloud account** and claimed **$300 in free**

credits.

Explored the **GCP Console and CLI** (gcloud). Learned about **pricing models** and **how to estimate costs**. Deployed a **Compute Engine VM** and installed a **web server**.

Next Chapter: GCP Core Services Overview

- Learn about **Compute, Storage, Networking, and AI services**.
- Understand **which services to use for different workloads**.
- Real-world example: How companies **choose the right GCP services**.

Let's keep building in the cloud!

CHAPTER 3

GCP Core Services – An Overview

3.1 Introduction: The Four Pillars of Google Cloud

Google Cloud Platform (GCP) provides **a vast range of services**, but at its core, **everything revolves around four key categories**:

Compute – Running applications, virtual machines, and containers.

Storage – Storing data, databases, and backups.

Networking – Connecting cloud resources securely and efficiently.

Security – Protecting applications and data from cyber threats.

Why Understanding Core Services Matters

- Helps you **choose the right service for your use case**.
- Avoids **unnecessary costs** by using the right level of abstraction.
- Improves **scalability and reliability** of your applications.

By the end of this chapter, you'll have **a high-level understanding of GCP's core services** and how to compare them with **AWS and Azure equivalents**.

3.2 Compute Services: Running Applications on GCP

GCP offers **multiple compute options** depending on your needs.

Service	Description	Use Case
Compute Engine	Virtual Machines (VMs)	Full control over OS and networking (similar to AWS EC2, Azure VMs).
Google Kubernetes Engine (GKE)	Managed Kubernetes clusters	Deploy and manage containerized applications (similar to AWS EKS, Azure AKS).
App Engine	Fully managed serverless platform	Deploy applications without managing infrastructure (similar to AWS Elastic Beanstalk, Azure App Service).

Service	Description	Use Case
Cloud Functions	Event-driven serverless compute	Run lightweight microservices without managing servers (similar to AWS Lambda, Azure Functions).
Cloud Run	Serverless containers	Deploy containerized apps with automatic scaling (similar to AWS Fargate, Azure Container Apps).

Real-World Example: Compute Engine vs. App Engine

A startup building **a new e-commerce platform** chooses:

- **Compute Engine** for **running a database server** with full control over the OS.
- **App Engine** for **handling user authentication** without managing servers.

3.3 Storage Services: Managing Data in GCP

Storage in GCP is **highly scalable, durable, and secure**.

Service	Description	Use Case
Cloud Storage	Object storage for unstructured data (files, images, videos)	Similar to AWS S3, Azure Blob Storage.
Cloud SQL	Fully managed relational databases (MySQL, PostgreSQL, SQL Server)	Similar to AWS RDS, Azure SQL Database.
Firestore	NoSQL document database for fast app development	Similar to AWS DynamoDB, Azure Cosmos DB.
BigQuery	Serverless data warehouse for analytics	Similar to AWS Redshift, Azure Synapse Analytics.
Cloud Spanner	Global-scale, strongly consistent relational database	Unique to GCP (not directly comparable in AWS/Azure).

Real-World Example: Migrating an On-Premise Database to GCP

A **financial services company** moves from an **on-premise MySQL database** to **Cloud SQL** to reduce operational overhead, improve disaster recovery, and enable **auto-scaling** during high-traffic periods.

3.4 Networking Services: Connecting Applications Securely

GCP has **one of the world's fastest, most reliable networks**, running on Google's **global fiber-optic infrastructure**.

Service	Description	Use Case
VPC (Virtual Private Cloud)	Private, isolated cloud network	Similar to AWS VPC, Azure Virtual Network.
Cloud Load Balancing	Distributes traffic across multiple instances	Similar to AWS ELB, Azure Load Balancer.
Cloud CDN	Content Delivery Network for faster web access	Similar to AWS CloudFront, Azure CDN.

50

Service	Description	Use Case
Cloud VPN	Secure connection between on-prem and GCP	Similar to AWS VPN, Azure VPN Gateway.
Cloud Interconnect	High-speed direct connection to Google's network	Similar to AWS Direct Connect, Azure ExpressRoute.

Real-World Example: Improving Performance with Cloud CDN

A **news website** serving global audiences integrates **Cloud CDN** to reduce **latency by 60%** and handle traffic spikes efficiently.

3.5 Security Services: Protecting Applications & Data

Google Cloud places **security as a top priority**, ensuring compliance with **ISO, GDPR, SOC 2, and HIPAA**.

Service	Description	Use Case
IAM (Identity and Access Management)	Controls user permissions and roles	Similar to AWS IAM, Azure AD.
Cloud Armor	DDoS protection and firewall	Similar to AWS Shield, Azure DDoS Protection.
Security Command Center	Detects threats across your cloud environment	Similar to AWS Security Hub, Azure Security Center.
Secret Manager	Securely stores API keys and passwords	Similar to AWS Secrets Manager, Azure Key Vault.
Cloud Audit Logs	Tracks security events and access logs	Similar to AWS CloudTrail, Azure Monitor.

Real-World Example: Enhancing Security for a FinTech Startup

A **FinTech company** storing sensitive user data uses:

- **IAM** to enforce **least privilege access** for developers.

52

- **Cloud Armor** to prevent **DDoS attacks** on its APIs.
- **Secret Manager** to secure API keys **instead of hardcoding them in applications**.

3.6 Comparing GCP to AWS and Azure

If you're **familiar with AWS or Azure**, here's a **quick comparison of equivalent services**:

Service Type	Google Cloud (GCP)	Amazon Web Services (AWS)	Microsoft Azure
Compute	Compute Engine	EC2	Virtual Machines
Serverless	Cloud Functions, Cloud Run	Lambda, Fargate	Azure Functions, Container Apps
Kubernetes	GKE (Google Kubernetes Engine)	EKS (Elastic Kubernetes Service)	AKS (Azure Kubernetes Service)
Object Storage	Cloud Storage	S3	Blob Storage

Service Type	Google Cloud (GCP)	Amazon Web Services (AWS)	Microsoft Azure
SQL Databases	Cloud SQL	RDS	Azure SQL Database
NoSQL Databases	Firestore, Bigtable	DynamoDB	Cosmos DB
Data Warehouse	BigQuery	Redshift	Synapse Analytics
Networking	VPC	VPC	Virtual Network
Load Balancing	Cloud Load Balancer	ELB	Load Balancer
CDN	Cloud CDN	CloudFront	Azure CDN
Security & IAM	IAM, Cloud Armor	IAM, Shield	Azure AD, DDoS Protection

Key Takeaway: GCP excels in **AI/ML, big data, and Kubernetes**, while **AWS has the largest service catalog, and Azure is best for Microsoft-centric environments**.

3.7 Real-World Example: A Company Migrating to GCP

A **mid-sized e-commerce company** is struggling with: **High operational costs** maintaining physical servers. **Scalability issues** during seasonal shopping events. **Slow performance** due to data center limitations.

How GCP Solves These Issues:

Moves their **application to App Engine** for **auto-scaling and cost optimization**. Uses **Cloud SQL** to **manage databases without manual backups**. Implements **Cloud CDN** to **serve product images faster globally**. Uses **BigQuery** for **real-time sales analytics and demand forecasting**.

Result: 30% cost savings, 50% improvement in site performance, and faster response times during peak sales periods.

3.8 Summary: Choosing the Right GCP Service

- **Compute Engine** → Full control over VMs.
- **Kubernetes Engine** → Best for managing **containerized applications**.
- **Cloud Storage** → Store **files, images, and backups**.
- **BigQuery** → **Analyze large datasets quickly**.
- **IAM & Security Services** → **Protect applications and data**.

Next Chapter: IAM & Access Control in GCP

- Learn how to **manage users, roles, and permissions**.
- Secure **API keys, service accounts, and Cloud Identity**.
- Hands-on example: Setting up IAM policies for a team.

Let's build a secure cloud environment!

CHAPTER 4

Understanding IAM (Identity and Access Management) in Google Cloud

4.1 Introduction: What is IAM and Why Does It Matter?

Identity and Access Management (IAM) is **the foundation of security** in Google Cloud Platform (GCP). It controls **who can access what** and **what actions they can perform**.

Why IAM is Critical for Security:

- Prevents **unauthorized access** to cloud resources.
- Ensures **users and services only have the permissions they need**.
- Helps with **compliance** (GDPR, SOC 2, HIPAA).
- Reduces security risks by enforcing **least privilege access**.

In this chapter, you'll learn: **How IAM works in GCP** and how to manage users and permissions.

The difference between users, roles, and service accounts.

How to apply best practices like least privilege access.

Hands-on tutorial: Creating IAM policies for a multi-team project.

By the end of this chapter, you'll have a **secure IAM setup** for your Google Cloud environment.

4.2 How IAM Works in GCP

Key Components of IAM

Principals (Who?) → Users, groups, service accounts, and workloads.

Resources (What?) → Compute Engine VMs, Cloud Storage Buckets, Databases.

Roles (How?) → Permissions that define what actions can be performed.

IAM follows a **hierarchical structure**:

scss

```
Organization (Company Level)
    ├── Folders (Departments)
    │       ├── Projects (Apps, Services)
    │       │       ├── Resources (VMs, Databases,
Buckets)
```

Permissions are inherited → If a user has access at the **folder level**, they automatically have access to all **projects and resources inside it**.

Key Takeaway: Assign **permissions at the highest logical level** to simplify management.

4.3 Managing Users, Roles, and Permissions

Users & Groups

IAM users are **individual Google accounts** (email@gmail.com or user@company.com).

Best Practices for User Management: Use **Google Groups** to manage permissions for teams (e.g., dev-team@company.com).

Assign **roles to groups, not individuals**, for easier management.

Roles in IAM

Roles define **what actions a user can take** in GCP.

Role Type	Description	Examples
Basic Roles	High-level roles that apply broadly	Owner, Editor, Viewer
Predefined Roles	Fine-grained access to specific services	Compute Admin, Storage Admin, Security Admin
Custom Roles	User-defined roles with specific permissions	A mix of permissions tailored to your needs

📖 **Avoid using Basic Roles (Owner, Editor, Viewer) because they are too broad**. Use **Predefined or Custom Roles** instead.

Service Accounts: Machine Identities

Service accounts are **special Google accounts** used by applications, rather than humans.

Used for **automation, API access, and inter-service communication**.

Each service account has **specific IAM roles** assigned to

60

control   access.
Service accounts use **keys (JSON credentials)** for authentication.

Security Best Practice: Never hardcode service account keys in your application—use **Workload Identity Federation** instead.

4.4 Setting Up Least Privilege Access (Best Practices)

Least privilege access means **only granting the exact permissions needed**.

Use Predefined Roles instead of Basic Roles. **Grant permissions at the lowest possible level** (resource → project → folder → organization). **Review and audit IAM policies regularly**. **Enable Cloud Audit Logs** to track permission changes.

Example: Assigning IAM roles for a web app team

Team Member Role

Developers	Compute Engine Instance Admin, Cloud Storage Editor
Database Admin	Cloud SQL Admin
Security Team	Security Reviewer, IAM Admin
DevOps	Kubernetes Engine Admin, Network Admin

Result: Developers can't modify databases, and security admins **can review but not modify IAM settings**— enforcing least privilege access.

4.5 Hands-On: Creating IAM Policies for a Multi-Team Project

Let's create **IAM policies for a real-world project** with **developers, database admins, and security engineers**.

Step 1: Create a New Project

Open **Google Cloud Console** → Navigate to **IAM & Admin** > **Manage Resources**. Click **Create Project**, name it `multi-team-project`, and click **Create**.

Step 2: Add Users and Assign Roles

Go to **IAM & Admin** > **IAM**. Click **"Add"**, enter the email (`dev-team@company.com`). Assign **"Compute Engine Admin"** and **"Cloud Storage Editor"**.
Click **Save**.

Repeat this for:
Database Admins → Assign **Cloud SQL Admin** role.
Security Engineers → Assign **Security Reviewer** role.

Step 3: Create a Service Account

Navigate to **IAM & Admin** > **Service Accounts**. Click **Create Service Account**, name it `backend-service`. Assign **"Cloud Run Invoker"** role to allow API calls. Click **Done**.

Now, your backend service has secure access without needing user credentials!

4.6 Summary: Securing Your Google Cloud Access

IAM is the backbone of security in Google Cloud—it controls who can access resources and what they can do. **Roles grant permissions**—use **predefined or custom roles** instead of broad basic roles. **Service accounts allow applications to authenticate securely**—avoid hardcoding credentials. **Use least privilege access**—only grant the minimum required permissions.

Next Chapter: Deploying Secure Applications on GCP

- Best practices for securing **APIs, storage, and databases**.
- Implementing **firewalls, encryption, and identity-aware proxy**.
- Hands-on: **Securing a web application** in Google Cloud.

Let's build securely in the cloud!

CHAPTER 5

Compute Engine – Virtual Machines on GCP

5.1 Introduction to Compute Engine

Google Cloud's **Compute Engine** provides **scalable, customizable virtual machines (VMs)** that allow developers to run applications **without managing physical hardware**. Whether you need **a single instance** for testing or **a fleet of auto-scaling VMs**, Compute Engine offers the flexibility to **deploy workloads efficiently and securely**.

Why Use Compute Engine?

- **Customizable VMs** – Choose OS, CPU, memory, and disk size.
- **Scalability** – Autoscale VMs based on demand.
- **Load Balancing** – Distribute traffic across multiple instances.
- **Integrated Security** – Built-in firewalls, IAM, and encryption.

By the end of this chapter, you will:
Create and manage virtual machines on Compute Engine.

Implement autoscaling and load balancing for high availability.

Deploy a web server using Nginx on a Compute Engine VM.

5.2 Creating and Managing Virtual Machines on Compute Engine

Step 1: Creating a VM Using the GCP Console

Open **Google Cloud Console** → Navigate to **Compute Engine > VM Instances**.
Click **"Create Instance"**.
Configure the instance:

- **Name:** web-server
- **Region:** Choose the closest to your users (e.g., us-central1).
- **Machine Type:** e2-micro (Free-tier eligible).
- **Boot Disk:** Debian Linux (default).

- **Allow HTTP/HTTPS Traffic** (Firewall settings). Click **Create**.

Your VM is now running on Google Cloud!

Step 2: Connecting to the VM via SSH

In the Compute Engine console, find your instance. Click the **"SSH"** button next to it. A terminal will open inside your browser.

Run a test command:

```
sh
```

```
uname -a
```

This will display the Linux kernel version running on your VM.

5.3 Autoscaling and Load Balancing for High Availability

Why Autoscaling and Load Balancing?

- **Autoscaling** adjusts the number of VMs based on demand.

- **Load Balancing** distributes traffic to prevent overload on any single VM.

Step 1: Creating a Managed Instance Group (MIG)

A **Managed Instance Group (MIG)** automatically scales VM instances.

Go to **Compute Engine > Instance Groups** → Click **Create Instance Group**. Choose **Managed Instance Group**. Select **Template** → Create a new VM template with the required settings. Enable **Autoscaling** and set **Min: 1, Max: 5 instances**. Click **Create**.

Now, your VM instances will automatically scale up or down!

Step 2: Setting Up a Load Balancer

Navigate to **Network Services > Load Balancing** → Click **Create Load Balancer**. Choose **HTTP(S) Load Balancer**. Select **Backend Configuration** → Add the **Managed**

Instance   **Group**.
Select **Frontend Configuration** → Assign an **external IP**.
Click **Create**.

Now, incoming traffic will be evenly distributed across all instances.

5.4 Hands-On: Deploying a Web Server with Nginx on a VM

Now, let's **install and configure Nginx on our Compute Engine VM** to serve a simple webpage.

Step 1: Install Nginx on the VM

SSH into the VM using the **GCP Console or gcloud CLI**:

```sh

gcloud   compute   ssh   web-server   --zone=us-
central1-a
```

Update package lists:

```sh
```

```
sudo apt update
```

Install Nginx:

```
sh
```

```
sudo apt install nginx -y
```

Start the Nginx service:

```
sh
```

```
sudo systemctl start nginx
```

Step 2: Serve a Custom Web Page

Replace the default Nginx page:

```
sh
```

```
echo "Welcome to my Nginx web server on GCP!" |
sudo tee /var/www/html/index.html
```

Restart Nginx to apply changes:

```
sh
```

```
sudo systemctl restart nginx
```

Step 3: Access Your Web Server

Get the **external IP** of your VM:

```sh

```

```
gcloud compute instances list
```

Open a browser and visit:

```cpp

```

```
http://[YOUR_VM_EXTERNAL_IP]
```

 **You should see the message "Welcome to my Nginx web server on GCP!" displayed!**

5.5 Summary: Mastering Compute Engine

Compute Engine provides powerful, scalable virtual machines for running applications.
Managed Instance Groups enable autoscaling based on demand.
Load Balancers ensure high availability by distributing traffic across instances.
Deploying a web server with Nginx on a VM is a common use case for Compute Engine.

71

Next Chapter: Google Kubernetes Engine (GKE)

- Why use **Kubernetes for containerized applications**?
- Deploying **a containerized app on GKE**.
- **Scaling and managing Kubernetes clusters** on GCP.

Let's move to containerized deployments!

Part 2
Deploying Applications & Managing Workloads

CHAPTER 6: GOOGLE KUBERNETES ENGINE (GKE) – MANAGING CONTAINERS

6.1 Introduction: Why Kubernetes?

As applications grow in complexity, developers move from **monolithic architectures to microservices**, breaking applications into **small, independent services**. While this **improves scalability and flexibility**, it introduces new challenges:

How do you efficiently manage multiple containers?
How do you scale applications up and down automatically?
How do you ensure availability, self-healing, and seamless updates?

This is where **Kubernetes** comes in. Kubernetes (K8s) is an **open-source container orchestration system** that helps deploy, manage, and scale containerized applications effortlessly.

Why   Use   Kubernetes?
Automated Deployment & Scaling – Easily scale apps

based   on   load.

Self-Healing – Automatically restarts failed containers.

Load Balancing & Traffic Management – Ensures traffic

is   evenly   distributed.

Rolling Updates – Deploy updates without downtime.

Portable & Multi-Cloud – Works on any cloud provider or
on-premise.

By the end of this chapter, you will: Understand why Kubernetes is essential for modern applications.

Learn how Google Kubernetes Engine (GKE) simplifies container   orchestration.

Deploy and auto-scale a Node.js application on GKE.

6.2 Google Kubernetes Engine (GKE): Simplifying Kubernetes

Google Kubernetes Engine (GKE) is Google Cloud's **managed Kubernetes service**, handling **infrastructure, security, and scaling** so developers can focus on building applications.

GKE Benefits Over Self-Managed Kubernetes:
Fully Managed Control Plane – Google manages the Kubernetes master nodes.
Automatic Scaling – Auto-scales pods and nodes as needed.
Integrated Monitoring & Logging – Native integration with **Cloud Monitoring and Logging**.
Built-in Security – IAM roles, network policies, and identity-aware proxy (IAP).
Hybrid & Multi-Cloud Support – Use **Anthos** to run GKE across multiple environments.

Key Takeaway: GKE makes Kubernetes easier, allowing developers to focus on applications rather than cluster management.

6.3 Deploying a Simple Containerized Application on GKE

Step 1: Enable GKE and Create a Cluster

Enable the GKE API:

```sh
sh
```

```
gcloud services enable container.googleapis.com
```

Create a Kubernetes Cluster:

```sh
sh
```

```
gcloud container clusters create my-cluster --
num-nodes=3 --zone=us-central1-a
```

This creates a **3-node cluster** in us-central1-a.

Authenticate with the Cluster:

```sh
sh
```

```
gcloud container clusters get-credentials my-
cluster --zone=us-central1-a
```

Now, you can interact with the cluster using kubectl.

Verify Cluster Status:

```sh
sh
```

```
kubectl get nodes
```

You should see a list of worker nodes running in your cluster.

6.4 Hands-On Example: Deploying a Node.js App with Auto-Scaling

Step 1: Create a Simple Node.js App

Create a directory and initialize a Node.js project:

sh

```
mkdir node-app && cd node-app
npm init -y
```

Install Express.js:

sh

```
npm install express
```

Create `server.js` and add the following code:

javascript

```
const express = require("express");
const app = express();
const port = process.env.PORT || 8080;

app.get("/", (req, res) => {
```

78

```
  res.send("Hello from Kubernetes!");
});

app.listen(port, () => {
  console.log(`Server running on port ${port}`);
});
```

Create a `Dockerfile` for the application:

```
Dockerfile

FROM node:14
WORKDIR /app
COPY package.json .
RUN npm install
COPY . .
CMD ["node", "server.js"]
```

Build and tag the Docker image:

```sh
docker build -t gcr.io/[PROJECT-ID]/node-app:v1
.
```

Push the image to Google Container Registry (GCR):

```sh
docker push gcr.io/[PROJECT-ID]/node-app:v1
```

Now, your application is containerized and stored in **Google Container Registry**.

Step 2: Deploy the Application to GKE

Create a Kubernetes Deployment file (`deployment.yaml`):

yaml

```
apiVersion: apps/v1
kind: Deployment
metadata:
  name: node-app
spec:
  replicas: 3
  selector:
    matchLabels:
      app: node-app
  template:
    metadata:
      labels:
        app: node-app
    spec:
      containers:
      - name: node-app
        image: gcr.io/[PROJECT-ID]/node-app:v1
```

```
ports:
- containerPort: 8080
```

Apply the Deployment:

```sh
sh
```

```
kubectl apply -f deployment.yaml
```

This will deploy 3 replicas of the Node.js app.

Create a Kubernetes Service (service.yaml):

```yaml
yaml
```

```
apiVersion: v1
kind: Service
metadata:
  name: node-app-service
spec:
  type: LoadBalancer
  selector:
    app: node-app
  ports:
  - protocol: TCP
    port: 80
    targetPort: 8080
```

Apply the Service:

```sh
```

```
kubectl apply -f service.yaml
```

This creates a **LoadBalancer service** that assigns an **external IP**.

Check the external IP:

```sh
```

```
kubectl get service node-app-service
```

Open the IP in a browser:

```cpp
```

```
http://[EXTERNAL-IP]
```

🎉 **You should see "Hello from Kubernetes!" displayed in your browser!**

6.5 Scaling the Application with Horizontal Pod Autoscaler (HPA)

Enable autoscaling on the deployment:

```sh
```

```
kubectl autoscale deployment node-app --cpu-percent=50 --min=3 --max=10
```

Check autoscaler status:

```sh
```

```
kubectl get hpa
```

Now, Kubernetes will automatically add or remove pods based on CPU usage.

6.6 Summary: Deploying and Scaling with GKE

Kubernetes is essential for managing modern containerized applications. GKE simplifies Kubernetes by handling cluster management for you. Deploying a Node.js app on GKE is straightforward with Kubernetes YAML manifests. Horizontal Pod Autoscaler (HPA) enables dynamic scaling based on demand.

Next Chapter: App Engine – Serverless Application Hosting

- What is **Google App Engine**, and when should you use it?
- Deploying a **serverless application on App Engine**.
- **Auto-scaling and managing multiple versions of an app**.

Let's explore serverless computing!

CHAPTER 7

App Engine – Serverless Application Hosting

7.1 Introduction: What is App Engine?

As developers, we want to **focus on writing code** rather than managing servers. This is where **Google App Engine** comes in.

App Engine is a **Platform as a Service (PaaS)** that allows developers to deploy applications **without managing the underlying infrastructure**. It provides:
Automatic Scaling – Grows with your traffic demand.
Built-in Security – HTTPS, IAM, and DDoS protection.
Multiple Language Support – Supports Python, Node.js, Java, and more.
Zero Server Maintenance – Google manages the OS, networking, and scaling.

When Should You Use App Engine?

You want serverless hosting – No infrastructure management   required.

Your app needs automatic scaling – Easily handle traffic spikes.

You need a fast time-to-market – Deploy apps quickly.

App Engine is best suited for web applications, APIs, and microservices that need **high availability and scalability** without the hassle of managing servers.

By the end of this chapter, you will:
Understand how App Engine works and when to use it.
Deploy Python, Node.js, and Java applications on App Engine.
Learn from a real-world example of a startup scaling with App Engine.

7.2 Standard vs. Flexible Environment in App Engine

App Engine offers **two environments** based on the level of control you need:

Feature	Standard Environment	Flexible Environment
Startup Time	Fast (Seconds)	Slower (Minutes)
Scalability	Scales instantly	Scales gradually
Supported Languages	Python, Node.js, Java, Go, PHP	Any language using Docker
Custom Dependencies	Limited	Full control with Docker
Pricing	Pay per request	Pay per running instance
Use Case	Web apps, APIs	Apps with special requirements

Key Takeaway:

- Use **Standard Environment** for **quick deployments and auto-scaling**.
- Use **Flexible Environment** if you need **custom runtimes or long-running processes**.

7.3 Deploying a Python, Node.js, and Java Application on App Engine

Step 1: Enable App Engine & Create a Project

Enable App Engine:

sh

```
gcloud app create --region=us-central
```

Select a **region closest to your users** (e.g., us-central).

Step 2: Deploying a Python App on App Engine

Create a Simple Python Web App

Create a directory for the app:

sh

```
mkdir python-app && cd python-app
```

Install Flask (lightweight web framework):

sh

```
pip install flask
```

Create `main.py` and add the following:

```python
python

from flask import Flask

app = Flask(__name__)

@app.route('/')
def home():
    return "Hello from Google App Engine!"

if __name__ == '__main__':
    app.run(host='0.0.0.0', port=8080)
```

Create `app.yaml` (App Engine configuration file):

```yaml
yaml

runtime: python39
entrypoint: gunicorn -b :$PORT main:app
```

Deploy the app to App Engine:

```sh
sh

gcloud app deploy
```

Open the app in the browser:

sh

```
gcloud app browse
```

🎉 **Your Python app is live on App Engine!**

Step 3: Deploying a Node.js App on App Engine

Create a Simple Node.js App

Initialize a new Node.js project:

sh

```
mkdir node-app && cd node-app
npm init -y
```

Install Express.js:

sh

```
npm install express
```

Create `server.js` and add the following:

javascript

```javascript
const express = require("express");
const app = express();
const port = process.env.PORT || 8080;

app.get("/", (req, res) => {
  res.send("Hello from Google App Engine!");
});

app.listen(port, () => {
  console.log(`Server running on port ${port}`);
});
```

Create app.yaml:

yaml

```yaml
runtime: nodejs18
entrypoint: node server.js
```

Deploy the app:

sh

```sh
gcloud app deploy
```

Open in a browser:

sh

```
gcloud app browse
```

🎊 Your Node.js app is live on App Engine!

Step 4: Deploying a Java App on App Engine

Create a Simple Java App

Initialize a Maven-based Java project:

```sh
```

```
mvn archetype:generate -DgroupId=com.example -
DartifactId=java-app                          -
DarchetypeArtifactId=maven-archetype-webapp   -
DinteractiveMode=false
```

Create   `HelloWorldServlet.java`   in `src/main/java/com/example/` and add:

```java
```

```
import java.io.IOException;
import javax.servlet.http.HttpServlet;
import javax.servlet.http.HttpServletRequest;
import javax.servlet.http.HttpServletResponse;
```

92

```
public      class      HelloWorldServlet      extends
HttpServlet {
    @Override
    protected void doGet(HttpServletRequest req,
HttpServletResponse resp) throws IOException {
        resp.setContentType("text/plain");
        resp.getWriter().println("Hello      from
Google App Engine!");
    }
}
```

Create app.yaml:

```
yaml
```

```
runtime: java17
entrypoint: java -jar target/java-app-1.0.jar
```

Deploy the app:

```
sh
```

```
gcloud app deploy
```

Open in a browser:

```
sh
```

```
gcloud app browse
```

🎉 Your Java app is live on App Engine!

7.4 Real-World Example: How a Startup Scaled with App Engine

A **fast-growing e-commerce startup** initially hosted its **web backend on Compute Engine VMs**, but it faced issues: **Manual scaling required** during high traffic. **Server maintenance & updates** slowed down the team. **Security concerns** with outdated patches.

How App Engine Helped:

Moved APIs to App Engine Standard – No server maintenance.
Auto-Scaled Seamlessly – App Engine **automatically adjusted instances** based on demand.
Deployed Updates Easily – With **version control**, testing new features was simple.

Result: 50% faster deployments, zero downtime, and reduced costs.

Key Takeaway: App Engine is perfect for **startups and enterprises** that want **scalable, serverless hosting without operational headaches**.

7.5 Summary: Why App Engine is a Game-Changer

App Engine simplifies deployments – No need to manage servers.

Supports Python, Node.js, Java, and more – Ideal for web apps & APIs.

Automatically scales up or down based on traffic.

Version control lets you test features without downtime.

Next Chapter: Cloud Functions & Cloud Run – Serverless Computing

- When to use **Cloud Functions vs. Cloud Run**.
- Deploying **event-driven microservices**.
- Hands-on: **Building a serverless API with Cloud Functions**.

Let's explore serverless functions!

CHAPTER 8

Cloud Functions & Cloud Run – Serverless Computing

8.1 Introduction: What is Serverless Computing?

In traditional cloud computing, developers **manage virtual machines (VMs) or Kubernetes clusters**. But **what if you could just write code and let the cloud handle the rest?**

This is where **serverless computing** comes in.

What is Serverless?

- **No infrastructure management** – No VMs, no servers to maintain.
- **Automatic scaling** – Apps scale instantly based on demand.
- **Pay-per-use pricing** – You only pay when your code runs.

Google Cloud offers **two major serverless solutions**: **Cloud Functions** – Best for **event-driven tasks (microservices, webhooks, background jobs)**.

Cloud Run – Best for **running full containerized applications** with automatic scaling.

By the end of this chapter, you will:
Understand when to use Cloud Functions vs. Cloud Run.
Deploy an event-driven serverless API using Cloud Functions.
Run a containerized application on Cloud Run.

8.2 Cloud Functions: Event-Driven Computing

What is Cloud Functions?

Cloud Functions is a **fully managed serverless compute platform** for running event-driven functions in response to:
HTTP requests (REST APIs).
Cloud events (file uploads, database changes, messages in Pub/Sub).
Scheduled jobs (like a cron job).

Best Use Cases for Cloud Functions:
REST APIs – Build lightweight APIs without managing servers.
Data Processing – Process images, logs, or user data in the

background.

Event-Driven Workflows – Trigger functions when files are uploaded or database records change.

8.3 Deploying a Serverless API with Cloud Functions

Step 1: Enable Cloud Functions

Enable Cloud Functions API:

sh

```
gcloud              services              enable
cloudfunctions.googleapis.com
```

Create a directory for the function:

sh

```
mkdir my-function && cd my-function
```

Step 2: Write a Cloud Function in Node.js

Install dependencies:

98

```sh

npm init -y
npm install express
```

Create `index.js` and add the following code:

```javascript

const express = require("express");
const app = express();

app.get("/", (req, res) => {
  res.send("Hello from Cloud Functions!");
});

exports.helloWorld = app;
```

Create `package.json` (required for Node.js functions):

```json

{
  "dependencies": {
    "express": "^4.17.1"
  }
}
```

Step 3: Deploy the Function

Deploy the function to Google Cloud:

sh

```
gcloud functions deploy helloWorld --
runtime=nodejs18 --trigger-http --allow-
unauthenticated
```

Get the function's URL:

sh

```
gcloud functions describe helloWorld --
format="value(httpsTrigger.url)"
```

Open the URL in a browser:

cpp

```
https://YOUR_FUNCTION_URL
```

🎉 **You should see "Hello from Cloud Functions!" displayed!**

8.4 Cloud Run: Running Containerized Apps Serverlessly

What is Cloud Run?

Cloud Run is **a fully managed service** that runs **containerized applications** without managing infrastructure.

Why Use Cloud Run?

Runs any containerized app – Supports any language.

Automatic scaling – Scales up and down based on traffic.

Cheaper than Kubernetes – Pay only when the app is running.

Stateless and event-driven – Great for APIs and microservices.

Best Use Cases for Cloud Run:

- **Deploying APIs & microservices**.
- **Running machine learning models in production**.
- **Processing batch jobs on demand**.

8.5 Deploying a Containerized App on Cloud Run

Step 1: Create a Simple Node.js App

Create a directory for the app:

```sh
```

```sh
mkdir cloud-run-app && cd cloud-run-app
```

Install Express.js:

```sh
```

```sh
npm init -y
npm install express
```

Create `server.js`:

```javascript
```

```javascript
const express = require("express");
const app = express();
const port = process.env.PORT || 8080;

app.get("/", (req, res) => {
  res.send("Hello from Cloud Run!");
});

app.listen(port, () => {
  console.log(`Server running on port ${port}`);
```

```
});
```

Step 2: Create a Dockerfile

Create a `Dockerfile`:

```
Dockerfile

FROM node:18
WORKDIR /app
COPY package.json ./
RUN npm install
COPY . .
CMD ["node", "server.js"]
```

Build the Docker image:

```sh
docker build -t gcr.io/[PROJECT-ID]/cloud-run-app:v1 .
```

Push the image to Google Container Registry:

```sh
docker push gcr.io/[PROJECT-ID]/cloud-run-app:v1
```

Step 3: Deploy to Cloud Run

Enable Cloud Run API:

sh

```
gcloud services enable run.googleapis.com
```

Deploy the container to Cloud Run:

sh

```
gcloud    run    deploy    cloud-run-app    --
image=gcr.io/[PROJECT-ID]/cloud-run-app:v1    --
platform=managed --allow-unauthenticated
```

Get the Cloud Run URL:

sh

```
gcloud run services describe cloud-run-app --
format="value(status.url)"
```

Open the URL in a browser:

cpp

```
https://YOUR_CLOUD_RUN_URL
```

🎉 **Your containerized app is now running on Cloud Run!**

8.6 Cloud Functions vs. Cloud Run: When to Use What?

Feature	Cloud Functions	Cloud Run
Use Case	Event-driven, small tasks	Full applications, APIs, microservices
Infrastructure	Fully serverless, no setup required	Runs any Docker container
Languages	Node.js, Python, Go, Java	Any language inside a container
Scaling	Auto-scales per request	Auto-scales containers
Pricing	Pay per function execution	Pay per container runtime

Key Takeaway:

- Use **Cloud Functions** for **lightweight, event-driven microservices**.

- Use **Cloud Run** for **containerized applications and APIs**.

8.7 Real-World Example: Serverless Computing at a Startup

A **tech startup** running an AI-powered chatbot needed a **cost-effective way to deploy their API** without managing servers.

Before Cloud Run:

Used **Compute Engine** VMs for hosting. **Manual scaling** during peak traffic hours. **High operational costs** due to idle servers.

After Migrating to Cloud Run:

Automatic scaling – The chatbot **scaled instantly based on** user **demand**. **Reduced costs by 70%** – Paid **only when requests were made**. **Simplified deployments** – No infrastructure maintenance needed.

Result: Faster API response times, lower costs, and a fully automated deployment pipeline.

8.8 Summary: Why Serverless Computing is the Future

Cloud Functions is great for **event-driven microservices**. **Cloud Run** is perfect for **running containerized applications**.

Both services eliminate infrastructure headaches and enable **fast, scalable deployments**.

Next Chapter: Cloud Storage – Storing and Managing Data

- **Object storage vs. databases – When to use what?**
- **Storing files, images, and backups in Cloud Storage.**
- **Hands-on: Hosting a static website using Cloud Storage.**

Let's dive into cloud storage!

CHAPTER 9

CLOUD STORAGE – SCALABLE OBJECT STORAGE

9.1 Introduction: Why Use Cloud Storage?

Cloud Storage is Google Cloud's **highly scalable, secure, and cost-effective** object storage solution. It is designed for **storing and retrieving unstructured data**, such as:

Images, videos, and documents (e.g., user uploads in an app).

Static websites (host HTML, CSS, and JS files).

Backups and disaster recovery (store database dumps and logs).

Big data and analytics (store large datasets for processing).

Why Use Cloud Storage Over Traditional Storage?

- **Fully managed** – No need to worry about server maintenance.
- **Global availability** – Stores and serves files from multiple regions.

108

- **Security & encryption** – Data is encrypted at rest and in transit.
- **Pay-as-you-go pricing** – Pay only for storage used.

By the end of this chapter, you will: Understand how Cloud Storage works. Store and retrieve files using Cloud Storage. Use signed URLs for secure file access. Host a static website using Cloud Storage.

9.2 Understanding Cloud Storage: Buckets and Objects

Google Cloud Storage stores data in **buckets**, and each bucket contains **objects (files)**.

Key Concepts:

- **Buckets** – Containers for storing objects (like folders).
- **Objects** – Individual files stored inside a bucket.
- **Storage Classes** – Determines pricing and availability.

Cloud Storage Classes: Choosing the Right One

GCP offers **four storage classes** optimized for different use cases.

Storage Class	Best For	Retrieval Cost	Availability
Standard	Frequent access (e.g., web apps, streaming)	Low	99.99%
Nearline	Data accessed ~once a month (e.g., backups)	Moderate	99.95%
Coldline	Data accessed ~once a year (e.g., disaster recovery)	Higher	99.90%
Archive	Long-term storage (e.g., compliance, legal)	Highest	99.90%

Key Takeaway: Use **Standard** for frequently accessed files, **Nearline or Coldline** for backups, and **Archive** for long-term storage.

9.3 Storing and Retrieving Files in Cloud Storage

Step 1: Enable Cloud Storage & Create a Bucket

Enable Cloud Storage API:

```sh
```

```sh
gcloud services enable storage.googleapis.com
```

Create a new storage bucket:

```sh
```

```sh
gcloud storage buckets create my-bucket-name --location=us-central1 --storage-class=STANDARD
```

Upload a file to the bucket:

```sh
```

```sh
gcloud storage cp myfile.txt gs://my-bucket-name/
```

List files in the bucket:

```sh
```

```sh
gcloud storage ls gs://my-bucket-name/
```

Download a file from the bucket:

```sh
```

```sh
gcloud storage cp gs://my-bucket-name/myfile.txt .
```

🎉 **Your file is now stored and accessible in Cloud Storage!**

9.4 Using Signed URLs for Secure File Access

By default, Cloud Storage files are **private**. To **share files securely without making them public**, use **signed URLs** (temporary, pre-authenticated links).

Generate a signed URL for a file:

```sh
gcloud storage sign-url gs://my-bucket-name/myfile.txt --duration=10m
```

This generates a **secure link** that expires in **10 minutes**.

Use Case: Allow users to download private files (e.g., invoices, reports) **without exposing the bucket to the public**.

9.5 Hands-On: Hosting a Static Website on Cloud Storage

Cloud Storage can serve **static websites** without needing a web server!

Step 1: Create a Public Storage Bucket

Create a bucket with a unique name:

sh

```
gcloud storage buckets create my-website-bucket
--location=us-central1 --storage-class=STANDARD
```

Make the bucket publicly accessible:

sh

```
gcloud storage buckets add-iam-policy-binding
my-website-bucket \
    --member=allUsers                        --
role=roles/storage.objectViewer
```

Step 2: Upload Website Files

Upload your HTML, CSS, and JS files:

```sh
sh
```

```sh
gcloud storage cp index.html gs://my-website-
bucket/
gcloud storage cp style.css gs://my-website-
bucket/
gcloud storage cp script.js gs://my-website-
bucket/
```

Set an HTML file as the default landing page:

```sh
sh
```

```sh
gcloud storage website set gs://my-website-
bucket/ --main-page-suffix=index.html
```

Step 3: Get the Public URL of Your Website

Find your website URL:

```perl
perl
```

```
http://storage.googleapis.com/my-website-
bucket/index.html
```

🎉 **Your static website is now live on Cloud Storage!**

9.6 Real-World Example: How an E-Commerce Store Uses Cloud Storage

A **fast-growing e-commerce company** needed **a scalable way to store product images and user uploads**.

Before Cloud Storage:

Stored images **on their own servers** → **expensive and hard** **to** **scale**.
High traffic slowed down their website when loading images.

After Migrating to Cloud Storage:

Stored all images in Cloud Storage → No infrastructure to manage.
Used Cloud CDN + Cloud Storage → **Reduced image load** **time** **by** **60%**.
Implemented signed URLs → **Users securely download their purchase invoices**.

Result: Lower costs, faster performance, and better user experience.

9.7 Summary: Why Cloud Storage is Essential

Cloud Storage is the easiest way to store and retrieve files in the cloud. Supports multiple storage classes to optimize cost and availability.

Signed URLs allow secure access to private files. Cloud Storage can host static websites without a web server.

Next Chapter: Cloud SQL & Firestore – Managed Databases

- **When to use SQL vs. NoSQL databases.**
- **Deploying a relational database using Cloud SQL.**
- **Hands-on: Using Firestore for real-time NoSQL data.**

Let's explore Google Cloud's database solutions!

CHAPTER 10

Cloud SQL & Firestore – Managed Databases

10.1 Introduction: Choosing the Right Database in Google Cloud

Databases are at the core of every application. Whether you're **storing user data, transaction records, or real-time messages**, choosing the **right database** is crucial for performance and scalability.

Google Cloud offers **two primary database types**:
SQL Databases – Structured, relational data (e.g., MySQL, PostgreSQL).
NoSQL Databases – Flexible, schema-less data (e.g., Firestore, Bigtable).

How Do You Choose?

Feature	SQL (Cloud SQL, Spanner)	NoSQL (Firestore, Bigtable)
Structure	Table-based, relational	Document-based, flexible
Use Case	Transactions, structured data	Real-time apps, flexible schemas
Scalability	Vertical scaling (Cloud SQL), Horizontal (Spanner)	Horizontally scalable
Best For	Banking, e-commerce, SaaS apps	Chat apps, IoT, social media feeds
Example	Order processing system	Messaging system

By the end of this chapter, you will: Understand when to use SQL vs. NoSQL in Google Cloud.

Set up a Cloud SQL and Firestore database. Run SQL queries and Firestore document operations. See a real-world example of a mobile app using Firestore.

10.2 Cloud SQL: Managed Relational Databases

Cloud SQL is Google's **fully managed relational database service,** supporting:

MySQL – Open-source, widely used relational database.

PostgreSQL – Advanced SQL features with strong community support.

SQL Server – Best for enterprises using Microsoft stack.

Key Features of Cloud SQL:

Automatic backups & replication – Ensures data durability.

Managed updates & security – No manual patching needed.

Seamless integration with Compute Engine, Kubernetes, and App Engine.

10.3 Setting Up a Cloud SQL Database

Step 1: Enable Cloud SQL

Enable Cloud SQL API:

119

```sh
```

```sh
gcloud services enable sqladmin.googleapis.com
```

Create a Cloud SQL Instance (MySQL example):

```sh
```

```sh
gcloud sql instances create my-sql-instance \
    --database-version=MYSQL_8_0 \
    --tier=db-f1-micro \
    --region=us-central1
```

This creates a **MySQL instance** in us-central1.

Get the instance connection name:

```sh
```

```sh
gcloud sql instances describe my-sql-instance --
format="value(connectionName)"
```

Step 2: Create a Database & User

Create a database inside the instance:

```sh
```

```
gcloud sql databases create mydatabase --
instance=my-sql-instance
```

Create a new SQL user:

```sh
sh
```

```
gcloud sql users create myuser --
password=mypassword --instance=my-sql-instance
```

Step 3: Connecting to Cloud SQL

Connect using the MySQL CLI:

```sh
sh
```

```
gcloud sql connect my-sql-instance --user=myuser
```

Run SQL commands:

```sql
sql
```

```sql
CREATE TABLE users (
    id INT AUTO_INCREMENT PRIMARY KEY,
    name VARCHAR(100),
    email VARCHAR(100) UNIQUE
);
INSERT INTO users (name, email) VALUES ('John
Doe', 'john@example.com');
```

```
SELECT * FROM users;
```

🎉 Your SQL database is now set up and ready to use!

10.4 Firestore: NoSQL Database for Real-Time Apps

Firestore is Google Cloud's **serverless NoSQL document database**, optimized for **real-time updates**.

Firestore   **Benefits:**
Real-time syncing – Great for chat apps and live updates.
No schema needed – Store JSON-like documents.
Fully managed – Google handles scaling, replication, and security.

Firestore vs. Realtime Database:

- **Firestore** → Best for scalable cloud applications.
- **Realtime Database** → Best for simple, low-latency mobile apps.

10.5 Setting Up Firestore and Running Queries

Step 1: Enable Firestore

Enable Firestore API:

sh

```
gcloud services enable firestore.googleapis.com
```

Create a Firestore database:

sh

```
gcloud firestore databases create --location=us-
central
```

Firestore is now ready for use.

Step 2: Adding Data to Firestore

Add a document to Firestore using the CLI:

sh

```
gcloud firestore documents create users/johnDoe
\
    --fields="name=John
Doe,email=john@example.com,age=30"
```

Retrieve the document:

```sh
sh
```

```sh
gcloud firestore documents get users/johnDoe
```

Firestore stores JSON-like documents in collections.

Step 3: Querying Firestore with Python

Install Firestore SDK:

```sh
sh
```

```sh
pip install google-cloud-firestore
```

Python script to fetch user data:

```python
python

from google.cloud import firestore

db = firestore.Client()

users_ref = db.collection('users')
docs = users_ref.get()

for doc in docs:
```

```
print(f"{doc.id} => {doc.to_dict()}")
```

🎊 **Firestore is now storing and retrieving real-time data!**

10.6 Real-World Example: A Mobile App Using Firestore

A **social media startup** needed a **real-time chat system** where messages **instantly appear** across devices.

Before Firestore:

Used **SQL databases** → Queries slowed down as messages increased.
Needed manual scaling to handle traffic spikes.

After Moving to Firestore:

Real-time sync – Messages instantly update across devices.
No infrastructure to manage – Google automatically scales.
Better performance – Queries return in milliseconds.

Result: Lower costs, zero maintenance, and a real-time chat system!

10.7 Summary: Choosing Between Cloud SQL & Firestore

Use Cloud SQL if you need structured, relational data with **transactions**. **Use Firestore if you need real-time updates** and **schema-less** **storage**. **Cloud SQL supports MySQL, PostgreSQL, and SQL Server**, while **Firestore stores JSON-like documents**. **Both services scale automatically** and integrate with GCP's AI, storage, and compute services.

Next Chapter: BigQuery – Data Warehousing & Analytics

- **Understanding BigQuery's serverless architecture.**
- **Querying massive datasets in seconds.**
- **Hands-on: Running SQL queries on public datasets.**

Let's explore data warehousing and analytics!

CHAPTER 11

BigQuery – Analytics and Data Warehousing

11.1 Introduction: What is BigQuery and Why Use It?

In today's world, businesses generate **massive amounts of data** from web traffic, IoT devices, transactions, and customer interactions. Traditional databases **struggle to handle petabytes of data**, making analytics slow and costly.

Enter BigQuery – Google's serverless, highly scalable, and cost-effective data warehouse.

BigQuery Benefits:

- **Serverless & Fully Managed** – No infrastructure management.
- **Lightning-Fast SQL Queries** – Uses Google's distributed query engine.
- **Scales Automatically** – Handles terabytes to petabytes of data.
- **Low-Cost Storage & Processing** – Pay only for the queries you run.

- **Built-in Machine Learning** – Train models directly in SQL.

When to Use BigQuery?
Business Intelligence (BI) & Reporting – Analyze customer data in real time.
Data Warehousing – Store and query massive datasets.
Machine Learning & AI – Run AI models on structured data.

Log Analysis – Process and query logs from cloud applications.

By the end of this chapter, you will: Understand how BigQuery works. Run SQL queries on large datasets efficiently. Use public datasets for hands-on practice.

11.2 How BigQuery Works: A Serverless Data Warehouse

Unlike traditional databases, BigQuery **decouples storage from compute**, meaning:

- **Storage is columnar and optimized for fast retrieval.**

- **Compute (query processing) is fully managed and distributed.**

BigQuery Key Components

Datasets → Containers for organizing tables. **Tables** → Structured data storage (rows & columns). **Queries** → SQL-based analysis on large-scale data. **Jobs** → Asynchronous tasks (queries, data loads). **Billing Model** → Pay per **storage (GB)** and **queries (TB scanned)**.

Key Takeaway: Unlike traditional databases that charge based on CPU and memory usage, **BigQuery charges only for what you store and query**—making it **cost-effective for large-scale analytics.**

11.3 Running Your First BigQuery Query

Step 1: Enable BigQuery

Enable BigQuery API:

```sh
```

```
gcloud services enable bigquery.googleapis.com
```

Open BigQuery Console:

```
sh
```

```
gcloud alpha bigquery datasets list
```

This verifies that **BigQuery is enabled** for your project.

Step 2: Querying a Public Dataset

Google Cloud provides **free public datasets** that you can query in BigQuery.

Example: Querying the GitHub public dataset

```sql
sql
```

```sql
SELECT repo_name, COUNT(*) as num_commits
FROM `bigquery-public-data.github_repos.commits`
GROUP BY repo_name
ORDER BY num_commits DESC
LIMIT 10;
```

This query retrieves the **top 10 most active GitHub repositories** by commit count.

Run this query from the command line:

```sh
```

```
bq query --use_legacy_sql=false \
'SELECT repo_name, COUNT(*) as num_commits
  FROM                        `bigquery-public-
data.github_repos.commits`
  GROUP BY repo_name
  ORDER BY num_commits DESC
  LIMIT 10;'
```

Step 3: Loading Your Own Data into BigQuery

Create a new dataset in BigQuery:

```sh
```

```
bq mk my_dataset
```

Upload a CSV file to BigQuery:

```sh
```

```
bq load --source_format=CSV my_dataset.my_table
gs://my-bucket/data.csv
```

Check if the table is loaded:

```sh
```

```
bq show my_dataset.my_table
```

Your data is now available for SQL queries!

11.4 Optimizing BigQuery for Performance & Cost

Use Partitioned Tables for Faster Queries

Create a partitioned table:

```sql
```

```sql
CREATE TABLE my_dataset.sales_data (
    date DATE,
    revenue FLOAT64
)
PARTITION BY date;
```

Why? Partitioning ensures **queries scan only relevant partitions**, reducing costs.

Use Approximate Aggregations for Speed

Example: Using `APPROX_COUNT_DISTINCT()` for faster calculations:

sql

```
SELECT     APPROX_COUNT_DISTINCT(user_id)     AS
unique_users
FROM my_dataset.website_logs;
```

Why? Approximate functions **return near-accurate results faster** than exact aggregations.

Query Only Necessary Columns (Avoid SELECT *)

Example: Querying specific fields instead of SELECT *:

sql

```
SELECT user_id, page_views
FROM my_dataset.analytics_data
WHERE event_date = '2024-02-01';
```

Why? Only scan necessary columns to minimize query costs.

11.5 Real-World Example: E-Commerce Analytics with BigQuery

A **large e-commerce company** needed to analyze **millions of customer transactions** across different platforms.

Before BigQuery:

Used **traditional relational databases** → Queries took **hours** to process.
Expensive infrastructure with high maintenance costs.

After Migrating to BigQuery:

Queries ran in seconds instead of hours.
Lower storage costs – Paid only for **storage used and queries run**.
Real-time analytics – Combined BigQuery with **Looker Studio** for live dashboards.

Result: The company **increased revenue by 20%** using **real-time customer insights** from BigQuery.

11.6 Summary: Why BigQuery is a Game-Changer

BigQuery is a fully managed, serverless data warehouse optimized for large-scale analytics. **SQL-based querying makes data analysis accessible** to developers and analysts. **Performance optimizations like partitioning and approximate aggregations** reduce costs and speed up queries. **Real-world businesses use BigQuery for customer insights, fraud detection, and business intelligence.**

Next Chapter: Dataflow – Streaming & Batch Data Processing

- **Batch vs. real-time data processing.**
- **Building ETL pipelines with Apache Beam.**
- **Hands-on: Streaming data into BigQuery using Dataflow.**

Let's process large-scale data in real time!

Part 3

DevOps, Automation, and AI/ML on GCP

CHAPTER 12

VPC and Networking Basics

12.1 Introduction: Why Networking Matters in Google Cloud

Every cloud application relies on **secure, scalable, and reliable networking** to function properly. Whether you're running **a small web app** or **a global enterprise system**, networking **impacts security, latency, and availability**.

Google Cloud's Virtual Private Cloud (VPC) provides:
Full control over networking – Define custom IP ranges, subnets, and firewalls.
Multi-region scalability – Easily extend networking across multiple regions.
Security and Isolation – Keep your workloads private and secure.

What You'll Learn in This Chapter:

- **How Google Cloud VPC works** and why it's important.
- **How to configure subnets, VPNs, and peering for connectivity.**

137

- **A real-world example of a multi-region VPC deployment.**

12.2 Understanding Virtual Private Cloud (VPC)

What is a VPC?

A **Virtual Private Cloud (VPC)** is **a logically isolated network** where you run **Google Cloud resources** like Compute Engine VMs, Kubernetes clusters, and databases.

Key Features of Google Cloud VPC:
Global Scope – One VPC can span multiple regions.
Automatic Routing – Routes traffic between subnets without extra configuration.
Flexible Subnetting – Define **custom subnets per region**.
Private Communication – Use **Private Google Access** to connect to Google services without a public IP.
Secure Connectivity – Use **firewalls, VPNs, and peering** to control access.

12.3 Setting Up a Custom VPC with Subnets

By default, GCP provides an **auto mode VPC**, but for **better control and security**, it's recommended to **use a custom mode VPC** with manually defined subnets.

Step 1: Create a Custom VPC

Enable the Compute API (if not already enabled):

```sh
gcloud services enable compute.googleapis.com
```

Create a custom VPC:

```sh
gcloud compute networks create my-custom-vpc --subnet-mode=custom
```

This creates an **empty custom VPC** where we can define subnets.

Step 2: Add Subnets to the VPC

139

Create a subnet in `us-central1` region:

```sh
sh

gcloud compute networks subnets create my-subnet-
central \
    --network=my-custom-vpc \
    --range=10.0.1.0/24 \
    --region=us-central1
```

Create another subnet in `europe-west1` region:

```sh
sh

gcloud compute networks subnets create my-subnet-
europe \
    --network=my-custom-vpc \
    --range=10.0.2.0/24 \
    --region=europe-west1
```

Now, your VPC **has two subnets** in different regions.

Step 3: Configure Firewall Rules

By default, **Google Cloud blocks all incoming traffic** except SSH (`tcp:22`). Let's create a firewall rule to **allow HTTP/HTTPS traffic**.

Allow HTTP and HTTPS traffic:

sh

```
gcloud compute firewall-rules create allow-http
\
    --network=my-custom-vpc \
    --allow=tcp:80,tcp:443 \
    --source-ranges=0.0.0.0/0
```

Now, any instance in this VPC **can receive web traffic**.

12.4 Secure Connectivity: VPNs, Peering, and Interconnects

VPC Peering → Connects two VPC networks **within Google Cloud** for private communication. **Cloud VPN** → Securely connects **on-premise networks to GCP** using an **IPsec VPN tunnel**. **Cloud Interconnect** → Directly connects your **on-prem data center to Google Cloud** via a **private fiber link**.

Step 1: Setting Up VPC Peering

VPC Peering allows two **separate** VPC networks to communicate **privately**.

Peer `my-custom-vpc` with another VPC (`another-vpc`):

sh

```
gcloud compute networks peerings create my-vpc-
peer \
    --network=my-custom-vpc \
    --peer-network=another-vpc \
    --auto-create-routes
```

Now, both VPCs **can communicate without using public IPs**.

Step 2: Configuring a VPN for On-Prem Connectivity

Create a VPN Gateway:

sh

```
gcloud compute vpn-gateways create my-vpn-
gateway --network=my-custom-vpc --region=us-
central1
```

Create a VPN tunnel:

```sh
gcloud compute vpn-tunnels create my-vpn-tunnel \
    --region=us-central1 \
    --peer-ip=ON_PREM_PEER_IP \
    --ike-version=2 \
    --shared-secret=MY_SECRET
```

Now, **your on-premise network can securely communicate with GCP.**

12.5 Real-World Example: A Multi-Region Deployment Using VPC

A **financial services company** needed a **multi-region VPC setup**   to:
Serve users in North America and Europe. Ensure low-latency and redundancy. Securely connect with their on-premise data center.

Their Solution:

143

Created a global VPC with subnets in `us-central1` and `europe-west1`.

Set up VPC Peering to **allow inter-region communication**.

Used Cloud VPN to securely connect their on-prem **datacenter** to **GCP**.

Implemented firewall rules to allow only **specific application traffic**.

Result: Secure, low-latency networking across multiple regions while maintaining compliance with financial regulations.

12.6 Summary: Mastering Networking in GCP

Google Cloud VPC provides secure, scalable networking across regions.

Custom VPCs offer better control over **subnets, IP ranges,** and **firewall rules**.

Use VPC Peering, VPNs, and Interconnects for **secure hybrid connectivity**.

Real-world businesses use multi-region VPC setups for **high availability and compliance**.

Next Chapter: Load Balancing & Traffic Management

- Global vs. regional load balancing.
- Configuring HTTP, TCP, and SSL load balancers.
- Hands-on: Setting up a multi-region load balancer for high availability.

Let's scale our applications with load balancing!

CHAPTER 13

Cloud Load Balancing & CDN – Scaling and Speeding Up Applications

13.1 Introduction: Why Load Balancing Matters

Modern cloud applications need to be **highly available, scalable, and fast**. Whether you're serving **millions of users worldwide** or handling **highly dynamic workloads**, Google Cloud offers **Cloud Load Balancing (CLB) and Cloud CDN** to ensure **speed and reliability**.

Key Benefits of Load Balancing & CDN:
Ensures High Availability – Distributes traffic across multiple   servers.
Improves Performance – Routes users to the closest server.
Auto-Scales Applications – Handles spikes in traffic automatically.
Optimizes Cost – Reduces the need for over-provisioned infrastructure.

What You'll Learn in This Chapter: Types of Load Balancers in GCP and when to use them. How Cloud CDN reduces latency and improves speed. Hands-on: Deploying a global load-balanced website.

13.2 Understanding Cloud Load Balancing

Google Cloud Load Balancing (CLB) is a **fully managed service** that distributes **traffic across multiple instances or regions**.

Why is Load Balancing Important?
Prevents overload – Spreads requests across multiple servers.

Handles failures – If one instance goes down, traffic is routed to healthy ones.

Improves latency – Sends users to the **closest, fastest server**.

Types of Load Balancers in Google Cloud

Load Balancer Type	Best For	Traffic Type
HTTP(S) Load Balancer	Websites, APIs, mobile apps	Web traffic (HTTP, HTTPS)
TCP Proxy Load Balancer	Secure backend applications	TCP (non-HTTP)
SSL Proxy Load Balancer	Encrypted traffic	SSL/TLS workloads
Internal Load Balancer	Private network traffic	Internal apps & microservices
UDP Load Balancer	Gaming, media streaming	UDP-based services

Key Takeaway:

- Use **HTTP(S) Load Balancer** for websites.
- Use **TCP or SSL Proxy Load Balancer** for backend apps.
- Use **Internal Load Balancer** for **private networking**.

13.3 Setting Up a Global HTTP(S) Load Balancer

We'll deploy a **global load balancer** to serve a website **across multiple regions**.

Step 1: Create a Managed Instance Group (MIG)

Create an instance template:

```sh

gcloud compute instance-templates create web-template \
    --machine-type=e2-micro \
    --image-family=debian-11 \
    --image-project=debian-cloud \
    --tags=http-server
```

Create instance groups in multiple regions:

```sh

gcloud compute instance-groups managed create web-group-us \
    --template=web-template \
    --size=2 \
    --zone=us-central1-a
sh
```

```
gcloud compute instance-groups managed create
web-group-eu \
    --template=web-template \
    --size=2 \
    --zone=europe-west1-b
```

Now we have multiple instances running in two regions.

Step 2: Configure the Load Balancer

Create a health check:

```sh
```

```
gcloud compute health-checks create http http-
basic-check --port 80
```

Create a backend service:

```sh
```

```
gcloud compute backend-services create web-
backend \
    --protocol=HTTP --health-checks=http-basic-
check --global
```

Attach instance groups to the backend service:

```sh
sh
```

```sh
gcloud compute backend-services add-backend web-backend \
    --instance-group=web-group-us \
    --global
sh
```

```sh
gcloud compute backend-services add-backend web-backend \
    --instance-group=web-group-eu \
    --global
```

Create a URL map and forwarding rule:

```sh
sh
```

```sh
gcloud compute url-maps create web-map --default-service=web-backend
sh
```

```sh
gcloud compute target-http-proxies create http-lb-proxy --url-map=web-map
sh
```

```sh
gcloud compute forwarding-rules create http-rule \
    --global \
    --target-http-proxy=http-lb-proxy \
```

```
--ports=80
```

Now, traffic is distributed globally across both regions!

Get the external IP:

```
sh
```

```
gcloud compute forwarding-rules list
```

Open the external IP in a browser:

```
cpp
```

```
http://[YOUR_EXTERNAL_IP]
```

🎉 **Your website is now globally load-balanced!**

13.4 Accelerating Content with Cloud CDN

What is Cloud CDN?

Cloud CDN (Content Delivery Network) caches static content at **Google's edge locations worldwide** to: **Reduce Latency** – Users get content from the nearest cache.

Lower Bandwidth Costs – Fewer requests hit backend servers.

Improve Availability – Cached content stays online even if backend fails.

Step 1: Enable Cloud CDN

Enable Cloud CDN on your backend service:

```sh
```

```sh
gcloud   compute   backend-services   update   web-
backend --enable-cdn
```

Now, Cloud CDN will cache website content globally!

Step 2: Testing Cloud CDN Performance

Check if caching is working:

```sh
```

```sh
curl -I http://[YOUR_EXTERNAL_IP]
```

Look for the X-Cache header:

153

- `HIT` → Cached content served.
- `MISS` → Request went to the origin server.

How to Improve Cache Performance?

- Use **Cache-Control headers** to set expiration times.
- Store **static assets** (images, CSS, JS) in Cloud Storage for better performance.

13.5 Real-World Example: A News Website Using Cloud Load Balancing & CDN

A **global news website** needed a **high-performance, scalable solution** to handle millions of daily visitors.

Before Load Balancing & CDN:

Slow load times for users in different continents. **Frequent downtime** during traffic spikes. **High server costs** due to excessive backend requests.

After Using Cloud Load Balancing & CDN:

Traffic is distributed globally, ensuring **zero downtime**. **Website loads 50% faster** with **Cloud CDN caching static**

content.

Reduced infrastructure costs by **offloading requests to the cache**.

Result: Faster website, better user experience, and lower costs!

13.6 Summary: Scaling Applications with Load Balancing & CDN

Cloud Load Balancing distributes traffic across multiple instances or regions. **HTTP(S) Load Balancers are best for websites & APIs**. **Cloud CDN caches content globally** to reduce latency and bandwidth costs.

Real-world companies use these services to improve speed, reliability, and cost-efficiency.

Next Chapter: Identity and Access Management (IAM) in Google Cloud

- **How IAM controls access to cloud resources.**
- **Setting up least privilege access.**

- **Hands-on: Configuring IAM roles for a secure project.**

Let's secure our cloud infrastructure!

CHAPTER 14

Cloud Security Best Practices

14.1 Introduction: Why Cloud Security Matters

Security is a **top priority** when running applications in the cloud. With cyber threats on the rise, organizations must **secure their data, applications, and user access** to prevent breaches.

Google Cloud provides powerful security tools to protect workloads,   including:
Identity-Aware Proxy (IAP) – Secure application access without   VPNs.
Encryption (At Rest & In Transit) – Protect data from unauthorized   access.
Security Command Center – Detect and respond to security threats.

What   You'll   Learn   in   This   Chapter:
How IAP restricts access to cloud applications securely.
How   to   encrypt   data   at   rest   and   in   transit.

Hands-on: Using Google Security Command Center to enforce security policies.

14.2 Using Identity-Aware Proxy (IAP) for Secure Access

What is Identity-Aware Proxy (IAP)?

Identity-Aware Proxy (IAP) allows you to **restrict access to applications** based on **user identity and context**, **without needing a VPN**.

Why   Use   IAP?
Stronger Security – Blocks unauthorized users, even if they   have   an   IP   address.
No Need for VPNs – Secure remote access without complex   network   configurations.
Granular IAM Controls – Define who can access specific apps.

Step 1: Enable IAP for a Web App

Enable IAP API:

```sh
sh
```

```sh
gcloud services enable iap.googleapis.com
```

Assign IAM Roles (Grant users access to IAP-secured apps):

```sh
sh
```

```sh
gcloud       projects       add-iam-policy-binding
[PROJECT_ID] \
    --member=user:example@gmail.com \
    --role=roles/iap.httpsResourceAccessor
```

Restrict all non-IAP traffic:

```sh
sh
```

```sh
gcloud  compute  firewall-rules  create  deny-
external-access \
    --direction=INGRESS --priority=1000 \
    --action=DENY --rules=tcp:80,tcp:443 \
    --source-ranges=0.0.0.0/0
```

Now, only authenticated users with IAP permissions can access the web app!

14.3 Encrypting Data at Rest and In Transit

Encrypting Data at Rest

Google Cloud automatically encrypts data **before storing it on disk** using **AES-256 encryption**.

Options for Encrypting Data at Rest:
Google-Managed Keys – Default encryption (no extra configuration   needed).
Customer-Managed Keys (CMEK) – Encrypt data using **Cloud   KMS.**
Customer-Supplied Keys (CSEK) – Bring your own encryption keys.

Enable CMEK for a Storage Bucket:

```sh
sh
```

```
gcloud storage buckets create my-secure-bucket \
    --location=us-central1 \
    --encryption-key=projects/my-
project/locations/global/keyRings/my-key-
ring/cryptoKeys/my-key
```

Now, your storage bucket is encrypted with a custom encryption key.

Encrypting Data in Transit

Google Cloud encrypts data **in transit** using **TLS** (**Transport Layer Security**).

Enable HTTPS for a Load Balancer:

```sh
gcloud compute ssl-certificates create my-ssl-cert \
    --domains=mywebsite.com
```

Apply SSL to a Load Balancer:

```sh
gcloud compute target-https-proxies create https-lb \
    --url-map=my-url-map --ssl-certificates=my-ssl-cert
```

Now, all traffic to your website is encrypted via HTTPS.

14.4 Hands-On: Enforcing Security Policies with Security Command Center

What is Google Cloud Security Command Center?

Security Command Center (SCC) is **a centralized dashboard for monitoring and managing security risks** in Google Cloud.

What SCC Can Do:
Detect misconfigurations – Identifies open storage buckets, weak IAM policies, etc.
Monitor real-time threats – Detects malware, unauthorized access, and insider threats.
Enforce security policies – Helps organizations stay compliant with industry standards.

Step 1: Enable Security Command Center

Enable SCC API:

sh

```
gcloud                services              enable
securitycenter.googleapis.com
```

Assign Security Admin Role:

```sh
```

```
gcloud       projects       add-iam-policy-binding
[PROJECT_ID] \
    --member=user:example@gmail.com \
    --role=roles/securitycenter.admin
```

Now, SCC is ready to monitor security threats.

Step 2: Scan for Security Issues

List Active Security Findings:

```sh
```

```
gcloud   security-center   findings   list   --
organization=[ORG_ID] --format=json
```

Check for Open Storage Buckets:

```sh
```

163

```
gcloud        storage        buckets        list        --
format="table(name,                                location,
iamConfiguration.publicAccessPrevention)"
```

Disable Public Access to a Storage Bucket:

sh

```
gcloud storage buckets update my-secure-bucket -
-public-access-prevention=enforced
```

Now, your bucket is fully locked down against unauthorized access!

Step 3: Enable Security Notifications

Set up real-time alerts for security threats:

sh

```
gcloud pubsub topics create security-alerts
```

Subscribe to alerts:

sh

```
gcloud pubsub subscriptions create security-
alerts-sub \
   --topic=security-alerts
```

Now, you'll receive notifications whenever a security event occurs!

14.5 Real-World Example: Securing a Healthcare Application in GCP

A **healthcare company** needed to **secure sensitive patient data** while remaining **HIPAA-compliant**.

Before Implementing Cloud Security Measures:

Publicly accessible storage buckets – Risk of exposing sensitive   data.
No encryption – Data could be intercepted during transit.
Lack of identity controls – Employees had unnecessary access to resources.

After Applying Security Best Practices:

Enabled Identity-Aware Proxy (IAP) – Only authorized doctors & admins can access patient records.

Enforced encryption (CMEK & TLS) – All data is encrypted at rest and in transit. **Used Security Command Center** – Real-time alerts for security threats.

Result: Fully compliant, secure cloud infrastructure that protects patient data!

14.6 Summary: Securing Google Cloud Workloads

Identity-Aware Proxy (IAP) ensures only authorized users access cloud apps. Encrypting data at rest and in transit protects against breaches.
Security Command Center detects threats and enforces security policies.
Real-world companies use these best practices to secure sensitive data.

Next Chapter: Automating Security with DevSecOps

- **Integrating security into the DevOps pipeline.**
- **Automating vulnerability scanning in CI/CD.**

- **Hands-on: Implementing security policies with Cloud Build.**

Let's build security into DevOps workflows!

CHAPTER 15

CI/CD Pipelines with Cloud Build

15.1 Introduction: Why CI/CD Matters in Cloud Development

Continuous Integration and Continuous Deployment **(CI/CD) automates software development**, allowing teams to **test, build, and deploy applications efficiently**. Google Cloud offers **Cloud Build**, a **fully managed CI/CD service** that integrates seamlessly with other GCP services.

Why Use Cloud Build?
Fully Managed – No need to maintain Jenkins or other CI/CD servers.
Fast & Scalable – Build and deploy applications in parallel.
Secure & Compliant – IAM-controlled access and artifact tracking.
Integrates with GitHub, GitLab, and Bitbucket – Automate workflows easily.

What You'll Learn in This Chapter: **How Cloud Build automates CI/CD pipelines.**

How to integrate Cloud Build with GitHub and GitLab. Hands-on: Setting up CI/CD for a microservices app.

15.2 Understanding Cloud Build and CI/CD Pipelines

What is Cloud Build?

Cloud Build is a fully managed CI/CD service that **compiles, tests, and deploys applications**. It integrates with:

Source Code Repositories (GitHub, GitLab, Cloud Source Repositories).

Artifact Storage (Cloud Storage, Artifact Registry).

Deployment Services (Compute Engine, Kubernetes, Cloud Run, App Engine).

CI/CD Workflow in Google Cloud

Developer	pushes	code	to	GitHub/GitLab
Cloud	Build	triggers	a	build
Cloud	Build	tests	the	code

If tests pass, Cloud Build deploys to production

15.3 Setting Up Cloud Build for Automated Builds

Step 1: Enable Cloud Build API

Enable the Cloud Build service in your GCP project:

sh

```
gcloud services enable cloudbuild.googleapis.com
```

Give Cloud Build permission to deploy resources:

sh

```
gcloud     projects     add-iam-policy-binding
[PROJECT_ID] \
    --
member=serviceAccount:[PROJECT_NUMBER]@cloudbui
ld.gserviceaccount.com \
    --role=roles/editor
```

Cloud Build is now ready for use!

Step 2: Create a Cloud Build Pipeline

Cloud Build uses **build config files (`cloudbuild.yaml`)** to define CI/CD workflows.

Example: `cloudbuild.yaml` to Build a Docker Image

yaml

```
steps:
- name: 'gcr.io/cloud-builders/docker'
  args: ['build', '-t', 'gcr.io/$PROJECT_ID/my-app:$SHORT_SHA', '.']

- name: 'gcr.io/cloud-builders/docker'
  args:     ['push',     'gcr.io/$PROJECT_ID/my-app:$SHORT_SHA']

images:
- 'gcr.io/$PROJECT_ID/my-app:$SHORT_SHA'
```

Trigger a manual build:

sh

```
gcloud builds submit --config=cloudbuild.yaml
```

This builds and pushes the Docker image to Google Container Registry (GCR).

15.4 Integrating Cloud Build with GitHub and GitLab

Step 1: Connect GitHub to Cloud Build

Authorize GitHub with Cloud Build:

sh

```
gcloud services enable cloudbuild.googleapis.com
gcloud                services                enable
cloudbuildtrigger.googleapis.com
```

Create a GitHub trigger:

sh

```
gcloud beta builds triggers create github \
    --name=my-ci-trigger \
    --repo-owner=my-github-username \
    --repo-name=my-repository \
    --branch-pattern=main \
    --build-config=cloudbuild.yaml
```

Now, Cloud Build will run automatically on every GitHub commit!

Step 2: Connect GitLab to Cloud Build

Enable the GitLab integration in Cloud Build:

sh

```
gcloud services enable cloudbuild.googleapis.com
```

Create a GitLab webhook to trigger Cloud Build:

sh

```
gcloud builds triggers create webhook \
    --name=my-gitlab-trigger \
    --secret=my-secret-key \
    --build-config=cloudbuild.yaml
```

Now, Cloud Build will trigger whenever code is pushed to GitLab.

15.5 Deploying a Microservices App with Cloud Build

Step 1: Define a Multi-Step Cloud Build Pipeline

Example: `cloudbuild.yaml` for Microservices CI/CD

yaml

```
steps:
```

```
- name: 'gcr.io/cloud-builders/docker'
  args:            ['build',            '-t',
'gcr.io/$PROJECT_ID/service-1:$SHORT_SHA',
'service-1/']
- name: 'gcr.io/cloud-builders/docker'
  args: ['push', 'gcr.io/$PROJECT_ID/service-
1:$SHORT_SHA']

- name: 'gcr.io/cloud-builders/docker'
  args:            ['build',            '-t',
'gcr.io/$PROJECT_ID/service-2:$SHORT_SHA',
'service-2/']
- name: 'gcr.io/cloud-builders/docker'
  args: ['push', 'gcr.io/$PROJECT_ID/service-
2:$SHORT_SHA']

- name: 'gcr.io/cloud-builders/kubectl'
  args: ['set', 'image', 'deployment/service-1',
'service-1=gcr.io/$PROJECT_ID/service-
1:$SHORT_SHA']
- name: 'gcr.io/cloud-builders/kubectl'
  args: ['set', 'image', 'deployment/service-2',
'service-2=gcr.io/$PROJECT_ID/service-
2:$SHORT_SHA']
```

This pipeline builds, pushes, and deploys microservices to Kubernetes (GKE).

Step 2: Deploy the Microservices on Google Kubernetes Engine (GKE)

Ensure Kubernetes cluster is running:

sh

```
gcloud container clusters create my-cluster --
num-nodes=3
```

Deploy the microservices:

sh

```
kubectl apply -f k8s/deployment.yaml
kubectl apply -f k8s/service.yaml
```

Check if deployments are successful:

sh

```
kubectl get pods
```

Microservices are now deployed on Kubernetes with Cloud Build automation!

15.6 Real-World Example: Automating Deployments for a Fintech Startup

A **fintech startup** needed an **automated CI/CD pipeline** for their banking app to: **Manually deploying updates took too long. Developers had to SSH into servers for every release. No automated testing, increasing risk of bugs in production.**

How Cloud Build Helped:

Automated Builds – Every commit triggered a **new Docker image build**. **Automated Testing** – Cloud Build ran **unit & integration tests before deployment**. **Zero-Downtime Deployments** – Cloud Build pushed updates to **GKE with rolling updates**.

Result: Faster feature releases, fewer errors, and an **automated, secure CI/CD process!**

15.7 Summary: Automating CI/CD with Cloud Build

Cloud Build automates code builds, testing, and deployment.

CI/CD pipelines improve speed, security, and reliability.

Integration with GitHub & GitLab enables automatic deployments.

Microservices apps benefit from Cloud Build's scalable automation.

Next Chapter: Infrastructure as Code with Terraform & Deployment Manager

- **Why Infrastructure as Code (IaC) matters.**
- **Deploying resources with Terraform on GCP.**
- **Hands-on: Automating infrastructure with Terraform.**

Let's automate cloud infrastructure!

CHAPTER 16

Terraform and Infrastructure as Code (IaC)

16.1   Introduction: Why Use Terraform for Infrastructure Management?

Manually provisioning cloud resources can be error-prone, time-consuming, and inconsistent. **Infrastructure as Code (IaC)** solves this problem by allowing developers to **define cloud infrastructure using code**.

Terraform is the leading IaC tool for managing infrastructure across multiple cloud providers.

Why Use Terraform?

- **Automates Infrastructure Provisioning** – No need for manual setup.
- **Consistent & Repeatable Deployments** – Define resources in code.
- **Works Across Cloud Providers** – AWS, Azure, GCP, Kubernetes, and more.

- **Tracks Infrastructure Changes** – Version control for cloud environments.

What You'll Learn in This Chapter:
How Terraform automates cloud infrastructure.
How to write Terraform configurations for Google Cloud.
Hands-on: Deploying a Kubernetes cluster using Terraform.

16.2 Understanding Terraform and IaC

What is Terraform?

Terraform is an **open-source Infrastructure as Code (IaC) tool** that allows developers to **define, deploy, and manage cloud infrastructure using declarative configuration files**.

Terraform Key Features:
Declarative Syntax – Define infrastructure in a simple, human-readable format.
Multi-Cloud Support – Works with **GCP, AWS, Azure, Kubernetes,** etc.

179

State Management – Tracks infrastructure changes to prevent drift.

Modular & Reusable Code – Use modules for reproducible deployments.

Terraform vs. Google Deployment Manager

Feature	Terraform	Deployment Manager
Cloud Support	Multi-cloud (GCP, AWS, Azure)	GCP-only
Language	HashiCorp Configuration Language (HCL)	YAML
State Management	Uses Terraform state file	No built-in state tracking
Adoption	Industry standard	GCP-native, but less flexible

Key Takeaway: Terraform is the preferred choice for managing multi-cloud and complex deployments due to its **flexibility, state management, and reusable modules.**

16.3 Setting Up Terraform for Google Cloud

Step 1: Install Terraform

Download Terraform CLI:

sh

```
curl                              -fsSL
https://apt.releases.hashicorp.com/gpg  |  sudo
apt-key add -
sudo   apt-add-repository   "deb   [arch=amd64]
https://apt.releases.hashicorp.com $(lsb_release
-cs) main"
sudo  apt-get  update  &&  sudo  apt-get  install
terraform
```

Verify installation:

sh

```
terraform version
```

Terraform is now installed!

Step 2: Authenticate Terraform with Google Cloud

Enable Google Cloud APIs:

```sh
gcloud services enable compute.googleapis.com
container.googleapis.com
```

Create a service account for Terraform:

```sh
gcloud iam service-accounts create terraform-
admin --display-name "Terraform Admin"
```

Grant permissions to manage resources:

```sh
gcloud projects add-iam-policy-binding
[PROJECT_ID] \
    --member="serviceAccount:terraform-
admin@[PROJECT_ID].iam.gserviceaccount.com" \
    --role="roles/editor"
```

Generate a service account key:

```sh
gcloud iam service-accounts keys create
terraform-key.json \
```

```
    --iam-account=terraform-
admin@[PROJECT_ID].iam.gserviceaccount.com
```

Now, Terraform can authenticate with GCP!

16.4 Writing Your First Terraform Configuration

Step 1: Create a Terraform Project

Create a project directory:

```sh
sh
```

```sh
mkdir terraform-gke && cd terraform-gke
```

Initialize Terraform:

```sh
sh
```

```sh
terraform init
```

Terraform is now ready to manage infrastructure!

Step 2: Define a Kubernetes Cluster in Terraform

Create a new Terraform configuration file (`main.tf`)

hcl

```
provider "google" {
  credentials = file("terraform-key.json")
  project     = "my-gcp-project"
  region      = "us-central1"
}

resource "google_container_cluster" "primary" {
  name     = "my-k8s-cluster"
  location = "us-central1"

  remove_default_node_pool = true
  initial_node_count       = 1
}

resource               "google_container_node_pool"
"primary_nodes" {
  name       = "my-node-pool"
  cluster                                          =
google_container_cluster.primary.name
  location   = "us-central1"
  node_count = 2

  node_config {
    machine_type = "e2-medium"
    disk_size_gb = 20
```

```
  oauth_scopes = [
    "https://www.googleapis.com/auth/cloud-
platform"
  ]
 }
}
```

This configuration creates a Google Kubernetes Engine (GKE) cluster with a node pool of two instances.

Step 3: Deploy the Kubernetes Cluster

Initialize Terraform:

```sh
sh
```

```
terraform init
```

Validate the configuration:

```sh
sh
```

```
terraform validate
```

Preview the deployment plan:

```sh
sh
```

```
terraform plan
```

Apply the configuration to deploy the cluster:

```
sh
```

```
terraform apply -auto-approve
```

Terraform will create the GKE cluster automatically!

Step 4: Verify the Kubernetes Cluster

Fetch the GKE credentials:

```
sh
```

```
gcloud container clusters get-credentials my-
k8s-cluster --region=us-central1
```

Check running Kubernetes nodes:

```
sh
```

```
kubectl get nodes
```

🎉 **Your Kubernetes cluster is now running on Google Cloud!**

16.5 Managing and Updating Infrastructure with Terraform

Scaling the Kubernetes Cluster

Modify `node_count` in `main.tf`:

hcl

```
node_count = 3
```

Apply the changes:

sh

```
terraform apply -auto-approve
```

Terraform will automatically scale the cluster to 3 nodes!

Destroying the Infrastructure

Delete all resources managed by Terraform:

```sh
```

```
terraform destroy -auto-approve
```

All cloud resources will be deleted automatically!

16.6 Real-World Example: Automating Infrastructure for a SaaS Company

A **SaaS company** needed to **automate cloud deployments** across multiple environments.

Challenges Before Terraform:

Manual VM provisioning – Engineers created instances manually.

Inconsistent environments – Staging and production were different.

Difficult rollback process – Infrastructure changes were risky.

How Terraform Helped:

Automated Infrastructure – Terraform defined everything in code.

Consistent Deployments – Staging and production were identical.

Easy Rollbacks – Changes were version-controlled and reversible.

Result: Faster, reliable, and secure infrastructure deployments across multiple regions.

16.7 Summary: Terraform for Cloud Automation

Terraform enables Infrastructure as Code (IaC) for scalable cloud management.
Declarative configurations define cloud resources in a repeatable way.
State management tracks infrastructure changes and prevents drift.
Terraform simplifies multi-cloud deployments across GCP, AWS, and Azure.

Next Chapter: Monitoring & Logging with Cloud Operations

- Setting up Cloud Monitoring and Logging.
- Automating alerts for application health.
- Hands-on: Monitoring a Kubernetes cluster in Google Cloud.

Let's keep our infrastructure healthy with monitoring!

CHAPTER 17

Monitoring & Logging with Stackdriver (Cloud Operations Suite)

17.1 Introduction: Why Monitoring & Logging Are Essential

In cloud environments, **monitoring and logging** ensure **application reliability, security, and performance**. Without proper monitoring, teams struggle to detect **failures, slow performance, and security threats**.

Google Cloud Operations Suite (formerly Stackdriver) provides:

Real-time monitoring & alerting – Detect failures before users   do.

Comprehensive logging – Collect, analyze, and store logs efficiently.

Traceability & Debugging – Find slow API responses and troubleshoot errors.

What You'll Learn in This Chapter:
How to set up Cloud Monitoring and create dashboards.
How to implement Cloud Logging best practices.
Real-world example: Debugging slow API responses
using Stackdriver.

17.2 Understanding Google Cloud Operations Suite

What is Stackdriver?

Google Cloud Operations Suite (formerly Stackdriver) is a set of tools for **monitoring, logging, tracing, and debugging applications** running on Google Cloud, AWS, or hybrid environments.

Key Components of Google Cloud Operations Suite:
Cloud Monitoring – Tracks metrics like CPU, memory, and   uptime.

Cloud Logging – Collects logs from applications and cloud resources.

Cloud Trace – Identifies slow API requests and latency issues.

Cloud Profiler – Optimizes application performance by detecting   bottlenecks.

Cloud Debugger – Provides real-time debugging for production apps.

Key Takeaway: Cloud Operations Suite provides a **complete monitoring and logging solution** for cloud applications.

17.3 Setting Up Cloud Monitoring and Alerts

Step 1: Enable Cloud Monitoring

Enable Cloud Monitoring API:

```sh
gcloud services enable monitoring.googleapis.com
```

Create a Monitoring Workspace:

```sh
gcloud alpha monitoring workspaces create --project=[PROJECT_ID]
```

Now, you can start monitoring Google Cloud resources.

Step 2: Create a Custom Monitoring Dashboard

**Open the Cloud Console and navigate to:
Operations Suite > Monitoring > Dashboards**
Click **"Create Dashboard"**
Add **Compute Engine VM CPU Utilization**
Click **"Save"**

Now, you have a real-time monitoring dashboard!

Step 3: Set Up Alerting Policies

Alerts notify **DevOps teams when something goes wrong**
(e.g., high CPU usage, database crashes, API failures).

Create an Alert Policy for High CPU Usage:

```sh

gcloud alpha monitoring policies create \
    --display-name="High CPU Usage Alert" \
    --condition-display-name="CPU above 80%" \
    --metric-
type="compute.googleapis.com/instance/cpu/utili
zation" \
    --threshold=0.8 \
```

```
--notification-channels=email:your-
email@example.com
```

Now, an alert will trigger if CPU usage exceeds 80%.

Test Alert with High CPU Load:

sh

```
stress --cpu 2 --timeout 60
```

An alert should appear in Cloud Monitoring.

17.4 Logging Best Practices for Production Apps

Step 1: Enable Cloud Logging

Enable Cloud Logging API:

sh

```
gcloud services enable logging.googleapis.com
```

List all logs in your project:

sh

```
gcloud logging logs list
```

View logs for a specific Compute Engine instance:

```sh
sh
```

```
gcloud logging read "resource.type=gce_instance"
--limit 10
```

Now, logs are collected and viewable in Cloud Logging.

Step 2: Create a Log-Based Alert

Trigger an alert when an error occurs in application logs:

```sh
sh
```

```
gcloud logging metrics create error-metric \
    --description="Monitor application errors" \
    --log-filter="severity>=ERROR"
```

Set up an alert notification for this log metric:

```sh
sh
```

```
gcloud monitoring policies create \
```

196

```
    --display-name="App Error Alert" \
    --condition-display-name="App    Logs    with
Errors" \
    --metric-
type="logging.googleapis.com/user/error-metric"
\
    --threshold=1 \
    --notification-channels=email:your-
email@example.com
```

Now, you will be alerted when an error appears in logs!

17.5 Debugging API Issues with Cloud Trace

Problem:

A developer notices that API response times are **too slow**, leading to **poor user experience**.

Step 1: Enable Cloud Trace

Enable the Cloud Trace API:

```sh
gcloud services enable cloudtrace.googleapis.com
```

List traces for a web application:

```sh

gcloud beta trace list
```

Analyze slow requests:

```sh

gcloud beta trace list --sort=latency
```

This will show slow API requests that need optimization.

Step 2: Identify the Bottleneck

Open **Cloud Trace** in the Google Cloud Console. Identify **slowest API calls** in the request timeline. Click a slow request and check **which function is causing the delay**.

Common API Performance Issues: **Slow database queries** – Use indexing to optimize performance.

High memory usage – Use Cloud Profiler to analyze CPU & RAM bottlenecks.

198

Unoptimized API routes – Optimize backend logic and caching strategies.

After fixing the issue, API response times improved by 50%!

17.6 Real-World Example: Monitoring a Global E-Commerce Platform

A **global e-commerce company** experienced **slow website performance** during high traffic periods.

Before Using Google Cloud Operations Suite:

No real-time monitoring – Issues were detected **after** customers   complained.

Slow error debugging – Engineers spent **hours** finding problems.

API timeouts – High traffic **overloaded backend services**.

After Implementing Stackdriver (Cloud Operations Suite):

Set up Cloud Monitoring – Engineers received **alerts before downtime occurred**.
Used Cloud Trace – Identified **slow API requests and optimized response times**.
Implemented log-based alerts – Developers were **notified of errors instantly**.

Result: Faster website, **20% fewer support tickets**, and **better user experience!**

17.7 Summary: Monitoring & Logging Best Practices

Cloud Monitoring provides real-time visibility into cloud infrastructure.
Cloud Logging centralizes logs for analysis, debugging, and security audits.
Cloud Trace identifies slow API requests and helps optimize performance.
Real-world companies use Stackdriver to prevent downtime and optimize applications.

Next Chapter: Cloud Functions for Event-Driven Automation

- Using Cloud Functions for serverless automation.
- Triggering functions with Cloud Storage, Pub/Sub, and HTTP.
- Hands-on: Automating image processing with Cloud Functions.

Let's automate workflows with serverless computing!

Part 4
Scaling, Optimization, and Career Growth

CHAPTER 18

Scaling Applications with AutoML and AI Predictions

18.1 Introduction: Why AI & ML Matter for Scalable Applications

Artificial Intelligence (AI) and Machine Learning (ML) **enhance modern applications** by enabling **real-time predictions, automation, and personalization**. Google Cloud provides **AutoML and AI APIs** that allow developers to **integrate machine learning without needing deep AI expertise**.

Key Benefits of Using AI in Cloud Applications:
Automates Decision-Making – AI models learn patterns and make predictions.
Personalizes User Experience – AI enhances recommendations and search.
Reduces Manual Effort – Automates tasks like image recognition, sentiment analysis, and fraud detection.
Scales Efficiently – AI services handle millions of requests seamlessly.

What You'll Learn in This Chapter:
How to integrate AI/ML predictions into web applications.

How AutoML enables machine learning without deep expertise.

Hands-on: Building a personalized recommendation system using AI APIs.

18.2 Understanding Google Cloud AutoML and AI APIs

What is AutoML?

AutoML allows **developers without machine learning expertise** to create **custom AI models** for:

- **Image recognition** (AutoML Vision)
- **Text analysis** (AutoML Natural Language)
- **Structured data predictions** (AutoML Tables)

Google Cloud AI APIs vs. AutoML

Feature	Google AI APIs	AutoML
Use Case	Pre-trained AI models	Custom AI models

Feature	Google AI APIs	AutoML
Setup Time	Fast (ready to use)	Requires training data
Best For	Quick AI integration	Custom ML applications
Examples	Vision API, Translate API	AutoML Vision, AutoML Tables

Key Takeaway: Use **Google AI APIs for instant AI capabilities**, and **AutoML for training custom models**.

18.3 Integrating AI Predictions into Web Applications

Step 1: Enable Cloud AI APIs

Enable AI APIs:

sh

```
gcloud services enable automl.googleapis.com \
    vision.googleapis.com \
    language.googleapis.com
```

Create a new AI-enabled project:

```sh
gcloud projects create my-ai-project
gcloud config set project my-ai-project
```

Your Google Cloud project is now AI-ready!

Step 2: Using the Vision API for Image Recognition

Install Google Cloud Client Library:

```sh
pip install google-cloud-vision
```

Create a Python script (`vision.py`) to analyze an image:

```python
from google.cloud import vision

client = vision.ImageAnnotatorClient()

with open("image.jpg", "rb") as image_file:
    content = image_file.read()
    image = vision.Image(content=content)
```

206

```
response = client.label_detection(image=image)
labels = response.label_annotations

for label in labels:
    print(f"Detected:           {label.description}
(Score: {label.score:.2f})")
```

Run the script:

```sh
sh
```

```
python vision.py
```

This script detects objects in an image using Google's AI-powered Vision API!

Step 3: Deploying AI Predictions in a Web App

Example: Integrating AI Predictions into a Flask Web App

```python
python
```

```
from flask import Flask, request, jsonify
from google.cloud import language_v1
```

```
app = Flask(__name__)
client = language_v1.LanguageServiceClient()

@app.route('/analyze', methods=['POST'])
def analyze_text():
    data = request.json
    text = data.get("text", "")

    document                                    =
language_v1.Document(content=text,
type_=language_v1.Document.Type.PLAIN_TEXT)
    response                                    =
client.analyze_sentiment(request={"document":
document})

    return                        jsonify({"score":
response.document_sentiment.score})

if __name__ == '__main__':
    app.run(host='0.0.0.0', port=8080)
```

Run the Web App:

```sh
sh
```

```
python app.py
```

Now, users can send text to `/analyze`, and the app will return AI-generated sentiment predictions!

18.4 Building a Personalized Recommendation System with AI

Use Case: Personalized Product Recommendations

A **retail company** wants to show **personalized product recommendations** based on a user's **past browsing and purchase history**.

Step 1: Train a Recommendation Model Using AutoML Tables

Prepare a dataset with user interactions:

csv

```
user_id,item_id,timestamp,event_type
101,501,2024-02-01T12:30:00,buy
101,502,2024-02-02T14:45:00,view
102,503,2024-02-01T18:15:00,add_to_cart
```

Upload the dataset to Cloud Storage:

sh

209

```
gsutil    cp    recommendations.csv    gs://my-
bucket/data/
```

Train an AutoML model:

```
sh
```

```
gcloud ai custom-jobs create \
    --region=us-central1 \
    --display-name=product-recommender \
    --dataset=my-
bucket/data/recommendations.csv \
    --model-type=TABLES
```

AutoML will train a machine learning model to generate recommendations!

Step 2: Using the Trained Model for Predictions

Deploy the model:

```
sh
```

```
gcloud ai endpoints deploy product-recommender -
-model=product-recommender-model
```

210

Make a prediction using AI:

```sh
gcloud ai endpoints predict product-recommender \
    --json-request='{"instances":    [{"user_id":
101}]}'
```

AI will return a list of recommended products based on user behavior!

18.5   Real-World   Example: AI-Powered   Movie Recommendation App

A **streaming platform** wanted to improve **user engagement** by recommending movies based on viewing history.

Before AI Recommendations:

Users had to manually search for content. No personalized recommendations. Low retention rate due to poor user experience.

After Implementing AI Predictions:

AutoML trained a recommendation model using historical user data. **Users received personalized movie suggestions. Engagement increased by 30%** due to relevant recommendations.

Result: Increased watch time, happier customers, and higher retention rates!

18.6 Summary: Scaling Applications with AI & AutoML

AI-powered applications provide automation, personalization, and real-time insights. AutoML enables developers to train custom ML models without deep AI expertise. Google AI APIs (Vision, Natural Language, Translate) offer instant AI capabilities. Real-world companies use AI to improve customer experience, automate processes, and scale applications.

Next Chapter: Serverless Computing with Cloud Run & Cloud Functions

- **Deploying serverless microservices with Cloud Run.**
- **Building event-driven applications with Cloud Functions.**
- **Hands-on: Running a REST API using Cloud Run.**

Let's go serverless with Google Cloud!

CHAPTER 19

Edge Computing & IoT on GCP

The Internet of Things (IoT) is transforming industries by enabling **real-time data collection, automation, and remote monitoring**. However, processing data **on the cloud alone** isn't always efficient—this is where **edge computing** comes in.

Edge Computing & IoT on Google Cloud allow developers   to:
Process data closer to the source – Reduces latency and bandwidth   usage.
Enhance security – Minimizes exposure of sensitive data.
Enable real-time decision-making – Ideal for smart homes,   healthcare,   and   manufacturing.
Seamlessly integrate with cloud AI – Use ML models on IoT data for insights.

What   You'll   Learn   in   This   Chapter:
How Edge Computing and IoT Core work together.

How to connect IoT devices to Google Cloud. **Real-world example: Building a smart home automation system with IoT Core.**

23.2 Understanding Edge Computing and IoT in Google Cloud

What is Edge Computing?

Edge computing processes data **closer to IoT devices** rather than sending everything to the cloud. This reduces **network congestion, latency, and processing costs**.

Where is Edge Computing Used?
Smart Homes – Real-time automation (e.g., adjusting thermostats).
Manufacturing – Detecting machine failures instantly.
Healthcare – Monitoring patient vitals in real time.
Autonomous Vehicles – Making split-second driving decisions.

What is Google Cloud IoT Core?

Cloud IoT Core is a **fully managed service** that allows developers to securely **connect, manage, and analyze IoT devices** at scale.

Key Features of IoT Core:
Device Connectivity – Securely connects millions of IoT devices.
Edge Processing – Runs ML models on **Google Cloud Edge TPU** devices.
Seamless Integration – Works with **BigQuery, Pub/Sub, and Cloud Functions**.
Device Management – Monitor, update, and control devices remotely.

Key Takeaway: Edge Computing processes IoT data locally, while Cloud IoT Core manages devices and sends processed data to the cloud.

23.3 Setting Up Cloud IoT Core for an IoT Project

Step 1: Enable IoT Core API

Enable IoT Core API in your GCP project:

```sh
```

```sh
gcloud services enable cloudiot.googleapis.com
```

Create an IoT Core registry to manage devices:

```sh
```

```sh
gcloud iot registries create my-iot-registry \
    --region=us-central1 \
    --event-notification-config=topic=my-iot-
topic
```

This registry acts as a hub for IoT devices.

Step 2: Connect an IoT Device to Google Cloud

Generate an RSA key pair for the IoT device:

```sh
```

```sh
openssl    genpkey    -algorithm    RSA    -out
rsa_private.pem -pkeyopt rsa_keygen_bits:2048
openssl rsa -in rsa_private.pem -pubout -out
rsa_public.pem
```

Register an IoT device with IoT Core:

```sh
sh
```

```sh
gcloud iot devices create my-iot-device \
    --region=us-central1 \
    --registry=my-iot-registry \
    --public-key
path=rsa_public.pem,type=RSA_PEM
```

Now, the device is securely registered in Google Cloud IoT Core.

Step 3: Sending Data from an IoT Device

Install the MQTT client library:

```sh
sh
```

```sh
pip install paho-mqtt
```

Python script to send temperature data to IoT Core:

```python
python
```

```python
import paho.mqtt.client as mqtt
import time
import json
```

```
mqtt_host = "mqtt.googleapis.com"
mqtt_port = 8883
topic = "/devices/my-iot-device/events"
device_id = "my-iot-device"

client = mqtt.Client(client_id=device_id)
client.tls_set("rsa_private.pem")
client.username_pw_set(username="unused",
password="your-jwt-token")
client.connect(mqtt_host, mqtt_port, 60)

while True:
    payload = json.dumps({"temperature": 25.5})
    client.publish(topic, payload)
    print(f"Sent data: {payload}")
    time.sleep(5)
```

Run the script to send IoT data:

```sh
```

```
python iot_publish.py
```

Now, the device sends real-time temperature data to IoT Core!

Step 4: Processing IoT Data in Google Cloud

Store IoT data in BigQuery for analysis:

sh

```
bq mk my_iot_dataset
bq mk --table my_iot_dataset.temperature_data
timestamp:TIMESTAMP,temp:FLOAT
```

Stream IoT data into BigQuery using Dataflow:

sh

```
gcloud dataflow jobs run iot-dataflow-job \
    --gcs-location              gs://dataflow-
templates/latest/PubSub_to_BigQuery \
    --region us-central1 \
    --parameters            inputTopic=projects/my-
project/topics/my-iot-
topic,outputTableSpec=my_iot_dataset.temperatur
e_data
```

Now, IoT data is stored in BigQuery for real-time analytics.

23.4 Real-World Example: Smart Home Automation with Google Cloud IoT

Use Case: A Smart Home Monitoring System

A smart home company wants to **automate home appliances** based on **sensor data** from IoT devices.

Before Using Cloud IoT Core:

No central way to manage IoT devices.
Data processing happened on devices, leading to slow automation.
Security issues in handling remote IoT control.

After Implementing IoT Core & Edge Computing:

Devices connected securely to Cloud IoT Core – central management & updates.
AI models processed sensor data at the edge – faster response times.
Google Pub/Sub & Cloud Functions automated home devices based on real-time data.

Result: Faster automation, better security, and improved user experience.

23.5 Summary: Scaling IoT with Edge Computing in Google Cloud

Edge Computing allows IoT devices to process data locally, reducing latency.

Google Cloud IoT Core enables secure, scalable device management.

Google AI enhances IoT by running ML models at the edge.

Real-world applications include smart homes, healthcare, and industrial automation.

Next Chapter: Google Cloud's Future – Emerging Tech & AI Innovations

- **Future trends in cloud computing.**
- **Quantum computing & AI-powered automation.**
- **How businesses can prepare for next-gen cloud technologies.**

Let's explore the future of Google Cloud!

CHAPTER 20

Cost Optimization & Billing Strategies in Google Cloud

20.1 Introduction: Why Cost Optimization Matters

Cloud computing provides **flexibility and scalability**, but without proper management, costs can spiral out of control. **Optimizing your Google Cloud (GCP) usage** ensures that you're getting **the most value** without overspending.

Key Benefits of Cloud Cost Optimization: Lower operational expenses – Reduce wasteful cloud spending.

Improve efficiency – Pay only for what you need.

Increase predictability – Avoid surprise bills.

Enhance performance – Optimize workloads for better performance at lower costs.

What You'll Learn in This Chapter: How Google Cloud's billing system works. Best practices to reduce cloud costs.

Hands-on: Using Google's cost estimator to optimize spending.

20.2 Understanding Google Cloud Billing

How GCP Charges for Services

Google Cloud follows a **pay-as-you-go model**, meaning you only pay for the resources you use.

Key Billing Components:
Compute Costs – Virtual machines (VMs), Kubernetes clusters, and App Engine.
Storage Costs – Cloud Storage, Persistent Disks, BigQuery.
Networking Costs – Egress data transfer, Cloud CDN, VPNs.
AI & Machine Learning Costs – AutoML, AI Platform predictions.

How to Avoid Unexpected Cloud Costs

Unused Resources: Idle VMs, orphaned disks, and unneeded snapshots.

Data Transfer Charges: Inter-region and external network traffic.

High-Performance Tiers: Using unnecessarily expensive machine types.

Key Takeaway: Monitoring your cloud usage **regularly** can prevent **unnecessary spending.**

20.3 Cost Optimization Best Practices

Use Preemptible VMs for Non-Critical Workloads

Preemptible VMs **cost up to 80% less** than standard VMs but can be **terminated by Google** if resources are needed elsewhere.

Create a preemptible VM:

```sh

gcloud compute instances create preemptible-vm \
    --machine-type=e2-standard-4 \
    --zone=us-central1-a \
    --preemptible
```

Best for batch processing, testing, and CI/CD jobs.

Choose the Right Machine Type for Workloads

List all available machine types to find the best fit:

```sh
gcloud compute machine-types list --filter="zone:us-central1-a"
```

Optimize by selecting cost-effective machine types (e.g., E2 series instead of N2 series).

Auto-Scale Compute Resources

Instead of **over-provisioning VMs**, use **autoscaling** to match demand dynamically.

Enable autoscaling on a managed instance group:

```sh
gcloud compute instance-groups managed set-autoscaling my-instance-group \
    --max-num-replicas=10 \
    --min-num-replicas=1 \
```

```
--target-cpu-utilization=0.6
```

Only pay for what you need at any given time!

---

se Cloud Storage Lifecycle Rules

Move **rarely accessed files** to cheaper storage classes like **Nearline or Coldline**.

Create a lifecycle policy to move objects older than 30 days to Nearline Storage:

```sh
sh
```

```
gsutil lifecycle set lifecycle.json gs://my-bucket
```

Example `lifecycle.json` policy:

```json
json

{
  "rule": [
    {
      "action": {"type": "SetStorageClass",
"storageClass": "NEARLINE"},
      "condition": {"age": 30}
```

```
    }
  ]
}
```

This reduces storage costs without losing data.

Use Committed Use Discounts (CUDs) & Sustained Use Discounts (SUDs)

Sustained Use Discounts (SUDs) – Get automatic discounts for continuously running VMs. **Committed Use Discounts (CUDs)** – Get **up to 57% off** by committing to 1- or 3-year contracts.

Estimate cost savings with a 3-year committed use discount:

sh

```
gcloud compute commitments create my-commitment \
    --plan=3-year \
    --machine-type=e2-standard-4 \
    --region=us-central1
```

CUDs are great for predictable workloads!

20.4 Hands-On: Using Google Cloud Pricing Calculator

Google's **Pricing Calculator** helps estimate cloud costs before deployment.

Step 1: Open the GCP Pricing Calculator

- Go to **Google Cloud Pricing Calculator**

Step 2: Estimate Costs for Compute Engine

1. Select **Compute Engine**
2. Choose a **machine type (E2-standard-4)**
3. Set usage to **730 hours per month (full-time usage)**
4. Compare **preemptible pricing**

Step 3: Estimate Costs for BigQuery

1. Select **BigQuery**
2. Enter **1 TB** of queries per month
3. Compare **On-Demand vs. Flat-Rate pricing**

Use this tool before launching large-scale workloads to estimate costs accurately.

20.5 Real-World Example: Reducing Cloud Costs for a SaaS Company

A **SaaS startup** struggled with **high cloud bills** due to:
Over-provisioned VMs – Running 30% more compute power than needed.
Expensive storage tiers – Keeping all backups in standard storage.
Unnecessary network traffic – Paying for unnecessary data transfers.

How They Optimized Costs:

Moved to Preemptible VMs – Reduced compute costs by 60%.
Applied Lifecycle Rules – Automatically archived old files to Coldline Storage.
Enabled Autoscaling – Eliminated idle resources and saved 35%.
Used Committed Use Discounts (CUDs) – Locked in long-term discounts.

Result: The startup cut **cloud costs by 50%** while improving system efficiency.

20.6 Summary: Smart Cloud Cost Optimization

Right-size your workloads – Choose appropriate machine types and autoscale.

Use Preemptible VMs – Drastically reduce costs for batch jobs.

Optimize storage costs – Move data to cheaper tiers using lifecycle rules.

Leverage sustained and committed use discounts – Save money on long-term workloads.

Use pricing calculators – Plan costs before deploying resources.

Next Chapter: Security & Compliance in Google Cloud

- **Implementing best security practices.**
- **Ensuring compliance with industry standards.**
- **Hands-on: Configuring security policies in GCP.**

Let's make cloud deployments secure and compliant!

CHAPTER 21

Incident Response & Disaster Recovery in Google Cloud

21.1 Introduction: Why Disaster Recovery (DR) Matters

Even the most reliable cloud infrastructure can experience **downtime, failures, or cyberattacks**. A well-defined **Incident Response and Disaster Recovery (DR) strategy** ensures that businesses can **recover quickly with minimal data loss**.

Why Implement a Disaster Recovery Plan?
Minimize Downtime – Keep systems running even during outages.

Protect Data – Ensure data remains safe in case of hardware failures or cyberattacks.

Meet Compliance Requirements – Essential for financial, healthcare, and enterprise organizations.

Improve Business Continuity – Avoid revenue loss and customer dissatisfaction.

What You'll Learn in This Chapter:
How to implement a robust Disaster Recovery (DR) plan.

Backup and failover strategies in Google Cloud.
Hands-on: Setting up automated backups and failover mechanisms.

21.2 Understanding Disaster Recovery Strategies

Four Levels of Disaster Recovery in Google Cloud

DR Strategy	Recovery Time Objective (RTO)	Recovery Point Objective (RPO)	Use Case
Backup & Restore	Hours to days	Hours to days	Archival, regulatory compliance
Pilot Light	Minutes to hours	Minutes to hours	Applications with periodic updates

DR Strategy	Recovery Time Objective (RTO)	Recovery Point Objective (RPO)	Use Case
Warm Standby	Minutes	Seconds to minutes	High-availability workloads
Multi-Region Active/Active	Instant	Near zero	Critical applications with 24/7 uptime

Key Takeaway: Choose the right DR strategy based on your business needs.

21.3 Implementing a Robust Disaster Recovery Plan in GCP

Step 1: Identify Critical Resources & Define RTO/RPO

Key Considerations:

- **Recovery Time Objective (RTO):** How long can your system be down?
- **Recovery Point Objective (RPO):** How much data loss is acceptable?
- **Business Impact Analysis:** Identify mission-critical applications.

Example:

A banking app requires **RTO = 5 minutes** and **RPO = 0 seconds** → Needs **Multi-Region Active/Active DR**.

Step 2: Set Up Automated Backups for Compute Engine

Enable automatic snapshots for VM disks:

```sh
```

```sh
gcloud compute disks snapshot my-disk --snapshot-names=my-disk-backup
```

Schedule daily backups using Cloud Scheduler:

```sh
```

```
gcloud scheduler jobs create pubsub daily-backup-
job \
    --schedule="0 3 * * *" \
    --topic=my-backup-topic \
    --message-body='{"action":"backup"}'
```

Now, VM backups will be created daily.

Step 3: Set Up a Failover Strategy for Compute Engine

Failover ensures that **if one region goes down, another region takes over automatically**.

Create a managed instance group with autoscaling:

sh

```
gcloud compute instance-groups managed create my-
mig \
    --base-instance-name=my-instance \
    --size=3 \
    --template=my-instance-template \
    --region=us-central1
```

Configure a global load balancer to redirect traffic during failures:

sh

```
gcloud compute url-maps create my-lb-map --
default-service=my-backend
gcloud compute target-http-proxies create my-
http-proxy --url-map=my-lb-map
gcloud compute forwarding-rules create my-lb-
rule --global --target-http-proxy=my-http-proxy
--ports=80
```

Now, traffic is automatically redirected to a healthy instance during failure!

Step 4: Set Up Cloud SQL High Availability (HA)

Create a highly available Cloud SQL instance with automatic failover:

sh

```
gcloud sql instances create my-db \
    --tier=db-custom-2-3840 \
    --region=us-central1 \
    --enable-binlog \
```

```
--failover-replica-name=my-db-replica
```

Check the failover status:

```sh
sh
```

```
gcloud sql instances describe my-db
```

Now, if the primary database fails, Cloud SQL automatically switches to the replica!

21.4 Real-World Example: Disaster Recovery for an E-Commerce Platform

Problem:

A **global e-commerce company** experienced downtime due to a **regional outage**, leading to **revenue loss and customer frustration**.

Before Implementing DR Strategies:

Single-region deployment – Entire app went down. **No backups** – Data was lost. **Slow recovery time** – Took **hours** to restore services.

After Implementing DR on Google Cloud:

Enabled multi-region failover – Traffic shifted to a secondary region instantly.

Automated database backups – Prevented data loss.

Implemented Cloud Load Balancing – Ensured high availability.

Result:

Zero downtime during outages, **increased reliability**, and **no lost sales!**

21.5 Summary: Ensuring High Availability & Resilience

Define RTO/RPO based on business needs.
Automate backups for Compute Engine and Cloud SQL.

Use failover strategies like Cloud Load Balancing & multi-region replication.

Real-world companies use DR to avoid revenue loss and ensure business continuity.

Next Chapter: Cloud Governance & Compliance in GCP

- Implementing security policies and IAM best practices.
- Ensuring compliance with industry standards.
- Hands-on: Configuring security monitoring in Google Cloud.

Let's secure and govern cloud resources effectively!

CHAPTER 22

Final Thoughts & Next Steps for Developers

22.1 Introduction: What's Next After Mastering Google Cloud?

Congratulations! 🎉 You've learned how to deploy, scale, and manage applications on **Google Cloud Platform (GCP)** using **DevOps, security best practices, AI, automation, and cost optimization**. But **cloud computing is constantly evolving**, and staying ahead requires **continuous learning and hands-on experience**.

Where do you go from here?
Get Certified – Boost your career with industry-recognized Google Cloud certifications.
Contribute to Open Source – Work on real-world projects to deepen your skills.
Join Developer Communities – Connect with cloud professionals for insights and networking.

Stay Updated – Follow trends in AI, serverless computing, and cloud security.

What You'll Learn in This Chapter: Certifications to advance your cloud career. Best open-source projects to gain hands-on experience. How to stay competitive in the fast-moving cloud ecosystem.

22.2 Getting Certified: The Best Google Cloud Certifications for Developers

Google Cloud certifications **validate your expertise** and make you stand out in the job market.

Which Certification Should You Choose?

Certification	Best For	Key Topics
Associate Cloud Engineer	Beginners	Deploying and managing cloud resources

Certification	Best For	Key Topics
Professional Cloud Architect	Experienced DevOps engineers	Designing scalable, secure applications
Professional Cloud Developer	Software developers	Building and deploying apps in GCP
Professional Cloud Security Engineer	Security professionals	IAM, compliance, data protection
Professional Data Engineer	AI & data professionals	BigQuery, ML, data pipelines

Steps to Prepare for Certification:
Take Google's Free Courses → Google Cloud Training
Use Qwiklabs for Hands-On Labs → Google Cloud Skills Boost
Read the Official Study Guides
Take Practice Exams
Schedule the Exam on Webassessor

Earning a Google Cloud certification can significantly boost your job opportunities and salary!

22.3 Contributing to Open Source & Real-World Cloud Projects

Best Open-Source Cloud Projects to Gain Hands-On Experience

Kubernetes (K8s) – Learn container orchestration by contributing to the K8s project.
Terraform Modules – Help improve cloud infrastructure automation.
Serverless Frameworks – Work on open-source projects using Cloud Functions.
BigQuery Datasets – Contribute to open-data projects for real-world analytics experience.

Where to Find Open-Source Cloud Projects?

- GitHub Trending: https://github.com/trending
- Google Open Source: https://opensource.google
- CNCF Projects: https://www.cncf.io/projects/

Contributing to open-source projects builds your reputation and strengthens your cloud expertise!

22.4 Joining Google Cloud Developer Communities

Best Communities for Cloud Developers

Google Developer Groups (GDG) → Find a local GDG

Google Cloud Community → Google Cloud Forums

Reddit: r/googlecloud → Discuss GCP use cases & best practices.

LinkedIn Groups & Discord Channels → Network with cloud professionals.

Cloud Conferences → Attend **Google Cloud Next**, **KubeCon**, and **DevOpsCon**.

Engaging with the cloud community helps you stay inspired, find mentors, and grow professionally!

22.5 How to Stay Ahead in the Cloud Computing Ecosystem

Keep Learning with Hands-On Labs → Use **Google Cloud Sandbox** for free-tier experiments.

Stay Updated on Cloud Trends → Follow **Google Cloud Blog** and **YouTube channels**.

Experiment with AI/ML & Serverless → Future-proof

your skills by learning **AutoML, AI APIs, and Cloud Run**. **Enhance Security Skills** → Understand **Zero Trust security models and compliance**. **Follow Cloud Thought Leaders** → Learn from top Google Cloud engineers on **Twitter, LinkedIn, and GitHub**.

22.6 Real-World Example: Building a Cloud Career from Scratch

Meet Alex – A Software Engineer Turned Cloud Architect

Before learning Google Cloud:

- Alex was a **backend developer** with no cloud experience.
- They struggled with **deploying scalable applications**.
- They felt **stuck in their career** and wanted **higher-paying roles**.

Steps Alex Took to Succeed in Cloud Computing: Earned the Associate Cloud Engineer certification to prove cloud expertise. **Built real-world projects** on Google Cloud using Terraform, Kubernetes, and CI/CD pipelines.

Contributed to open-source cloud projects to gain practical experience.

Joined Google Developer Groups (GDG) & attended cloud conferences.

The **Result?**

💰 **Landed a Cloud Engineer role at a major tech company.**

📈 **Increased their salary by 40%.**

🔝 **Became a mentor for aspiring cloud professionals.**

Cloud computing is a high-growth field—by learning and practicing consistently, you can accelerate your career too!

22.7 Summary: Your Next Steps in Cloud Computing

Get Google Cloud Certified – Boost your career and validate your expertise.

Contribute to Open Source – Gain practical experience in cloud projects.

Engage with Developer Communities – Learn from experts and network.

Stay Updated with Cloud Trends – Follow blogs, conferences, and thought leaders.
Keep Practicing & Building Projects – The best way to learn cloud is by doing.

Final Challenge: Build & Deploy a Full-Stack App on Google Cloud

- Use **Cloud Run, Cloud SQL, Firebase, and BigQuery**.
- Set up **CI/CD pipelines** with Cloud Build.
- Optimize costs using **Sustained Use Discounts**.
- Implement security best practices with **IAM & VPC**.

Congratulations! You're now ready to build, scale, and optimize cloud applications like a pro!